Contents

Acknowledgments

We particularly wish to thank Joshua A. Ederheimer, Acting Director; Matt Lysakowski, Senior Advisor for Tribal Affairs; and Erin P.T. Canning, Senior Technical Editor.

This publication was developed through the time and dedication of many people. We thank those who allowed us to interview them on numerous occasions. Those interviewed include the following:

Robert Brandenburg
Chief of Police
Lac du Flambeau Police Department
Lac du Flambeau Band of
Lake Superior Chippewa

Jada Breaux
Sergeant
Chitimacha Tribal Police Department
Chitimacha Tribe of Louisiana

Harold Comby
Captain
Choctaw Department of
Public Safety
Mississippi Band of
Choctaw Indians

John Cooper
Chief of Police
Fort Oakland Police Department
Tonkawa Tribe of Oklahoma

Marilyn Epley
Executive Planner
Tonkawa Tribe of Oklahoma

Ellen Hebert
Captain
Chitimacha Tribal Police
Department
Chitimacha Tribe of Louisiana

Scott LaFevre
Chief of Police
Coquille Tribal Police Department
Coquille Indian Tribe

John Leonard
Sergeant
Washoe Tribal Police Department
Washoe Tribe of Nevada
and California

William Loescher
Patrol Lieutenant and
Gang Supervisor
Puyallup Tribal Police Department
Puyallup Tribe

Kevin Mariano
Chief of Police
Isleta Police Department
Isleta Pueblo

Matt Ninham
Community Resource Officer
Oneida Police Department
Oneida Tribe of Indians
of Wisconsin

Vanessa Northrup
School Resource Officer
Fond du Lac Police Department
Fond du Lac Band of
Lake Superior Chippewa

Rodney Schurger
Sergeant
Kalispel Tribal Public Safety
Department
Kalispel Tribe

Blaise Smith
Chief of Police
Chitimacha Tribal Police
Department
Chitimacha Tribe of Louisiana

Lynn Soderquist
DOJ COPS Office Coordinator
Kalispel Tribal Public Safety
Department
Kalispel Tribe

Robin Souvenir
Chief of Police
Shoalwater Bay Police
Department
Shoalwater Bay Indian Tribe

Cecelia Stewart
Indian Education Mentor
Lakeland Union High School
Lac du Flambeau Band of
Lake Superior Chippewa

Rich Van Boxtel
Chief of Police
Oneida Police Department
Oneida Tribe of Indians
of Wisconsin

Richard Varner
Chief of Police
Washoe Tribal Police Department
Washoe Tribe of Nevada
and California

Warren Warrington
Master Sergeant
Menominee Tribal Police
Department
Menominee Indian Tribe
of Wisconsin

Kenneth Washington
Assistant Chief of Police
Leech Lake Tribal Police
Department
Leech Lake Band of Ojibwe

Wendell Willis
Director of Public Safety
Choctaw Department of
Public Safety
Mississippi Band of
Choctaw Indians

James Wynecoop
Director of Public Safety
Kalispel Tribal Public Safety
Department
Kalispel Tribe

Phil Zavadil
Director
Department of Community
Safety and Peace
Aleut Community of
St. Paul Island

The publication development team included representatives from the National Criminal Justice Training Center (Lynn Chernich, Project Coordinator; Anne Kinsey-Goldy, Consultant; Edward Krueger, Program Administrator (retired); Chelsea Iversen, Consultant; Kristina Mahloch, Project Coordinator; Patricia Robinson, Executive Dean, Public Safety; David Rogers, Tribal Public Safety Program Manager; and James Warren, Consultant) and the Fort McDowell (Yavapai Nation) Police Department (Mark Bach, Lieutenant). We would like to also thank the many reviewers and editors for their suggestions and guidance.

U.S. DEPARTMENT OF JUSTICE
OFFICE OF COMMUNITY ORIENTED POLICING SERVICES

Office of the Director
145 N Street, N.E., Washington, DC 20530

Dear colleagues,

On behalf of the Office of Community Oriented Policing Services, I would like to share my appreciation for the efforts the Fox Valley Technical College made to provide community policing training and technical assistance to tribal communities.

The successful delivery of the Tribal Community Policing Problem-Solving Teams (TTEAMS) curriculum to Tribal Resources Grant Program grantees has aided these law enforcement agencies in their advancement of community policing. The curriculum is focused on building partnerships in tribal communities to address local problems, which is the heart of community policing.

Successful Tribal Community Policing Initiatives: A Resource for Communities Developing Public Safety Programs and Strategies summarizes some of the most promising practices and results from the training events. The community policing strategies highlighted in this report address issues such as substance abuse, gangs, and forming partnerships, all of which are public safety issues that many law enforcement agencies face. The report also includes details on each promising practice, including outcomes and lessons learned.

A proud partner of this effort, the COPS Office hopes this report can help tribes and other law enforcement agencies address their public safety issues. This report, which is one of the first COPS Office publications to focus on tribal law enforcement, marks the beginning of a renewed effort to assist tribal law enforcement in advancing community policing through the development of additional guides and publications.

Sincerely,

Joshua A. Ederheimer, Acting Director
Office of Community Oriented Policing Services

Introduction

Background

The COPS Office introduced the Tribal Resources Grant Program (TRGP) to Indian Country in FY1999. Since the program's inception, the COPS Office has dedicated more than $300 million to TRGP to hire and train community policing officers and purchase new equipment and technology.

In FY2008, the COPS Office awarded the Fox Valley Technical College's National Criminal Justice Training Center (NCJTC) a cooperative agreement to provide training and technical assistance to the 75 tribes and agencies awarded TRGP funds that year. NCJTC helped these tribes and agencies enhance community policing by providing the Tribal Community Police Problem-Solving (TTEAMS) training and technical assistance in community policing and other public safety issues. (For additional information regarding the TRGP, visit www.fvtc. edu/TRGP.)

The two-day TTEAMS training course is intended to strengthen relationships between the community and tribal law enforcement agencies. Designed specifically for Indian Country by Native American community policing practitioners, the training brings together tribal leaders, youth, and elders as well as representatives from criminal justice agencies, local governments, social service agencies, educational organizations, and the community.

TTEAMS demonstrates how law enforcement and the community can work together in organized problem-solving teams to address key public safety issues such as crime, social disorder, and fear of crime by utilizing the community policing philosophy. The highly interactive training format encompasses various instructional methods including the principles of adult learning, group discussion, applied learning, team building, and interactive exercises. Throughout the training, students learn how to work together to identify problems and underlying conditions, leverage resources, and develop creative solutions.

In addition to the onsite TTEAMS trainings, NCJTC delivered specialized technical assistance to tribes on the following topics: alcohol and substance abuse, gangs, community partnerships, youth programs, and specialty programs, among others. This publication, which highlights successful strategies implemented by FY2008 TRGP recipients, is intended to serve as a resource for communities wishing to develop programs and strategies to improve public safety. The information contained for each of the highlighted tribal communities comes from interviews with the lead contacts listed for each community and the tribe's website.

What is Community Policing?

The Office of Community Oriented Policing Services (COPS Office) defines community policing as a "philosophy that promotes organizational strategies, which support the systematic use of partnerships and problem-solving techniques, to proactively address the immediate conditions that give rise to public safety issues such as crime, social disorder, and fear of crime."[1]

. . . .

1. *Community Policing Defined* (Washington, DC: U.S. Department of Justice, Office of Community Oriented Policing Services, 2012), http://ric-zai-inc.com/ric.php?page=detail&id=COPS-P157.

The community policing philosophy comprises three key components: community partnerships, organizational transformation, and problem solving. The first component, community partnerships, recognizes that public safety issues are rarely solved without the help of relevant stakeholders and partners.[2] Examples of important community partners include the following:

- Government agencies such as courts, probation and parole, corrections, schools, and social services

- Community members/groups such as volunteers, advocates, activists, residents, tourists, tribal elders, and formal or informal community leaders

- Nonprofits/service providers such as service clubs, support groups, community development corporations, faith-based organizations, and victims groups

- Private businesses, chambers of commerce, visitor centers, etc.

- Media such as newspapers, news stations, and social media sites[3]

The second component, organizational transformation, focuses on implementing organizational and management structural changes to ensure the philosophy of community policing is infused throughout the department, from management to patrol and civilian staff. Elements of organizational transformation can include agency management (e.g., climate and culture, leadership, labor relations, strategic planning, policies, evaluation, and structure); geographic assignment of officers; personnel (e.g., recruitment, hiring, and selection; personnel supervision and evaluation; and training); and information systems (i.e., technology).

The third component, problem solving, shifts the focus of responding to a crime after it occurs to developing proactive, creative solutions to address the underlying conditions.[4] The problem solving approach represents a change in the way law enforcement thinks about its work and also calls upon community members to contribute insight and ideas for the overall improvement of public safety. Agencies successful in implementing community policing use problem solving as a fundamental approach for officers and staff to carry out their functions and daily routines.[5]

A problem-solving model commonly used in community policing is SARA (scanning, analysis, response, and assessment). The scanning component includes "identifying recurring problems of concern to the public and police, identifying consequences, prioritizing problems, and determining how frequently the problems occurs and how long it has been taking place."[6] The analysis component includes "understanding underlying conditions, identifying relevant data that needs to be collected, researching what is known about the problem, and identifying resources that may be of assistance."[7] The response component involves "brainstorming new interventions, outlining a response plan, identifying responsible parties, identifying objectives for the response plan, and carrying out the activities."[8] The assessment component involves "process evaluation, collecting qualitative and quantitative data, determining whether the objectives were met, identifying any new strategies needed to adjust the original plan, and conducting ongoing assessment to ensure effectiveness.[9]

For an example illustrating the implementation of the SARA model, see the Kalispel Tribe's "Strategy to Address Crime" on page 68.

. . . .

2. Ibid.

3. Ibid.

4. Ibid.

5. Edward Maguire and William Wells, eds., *Implementing Community Policing: Lessons from 12 Agencies* (Washington, DC: U.S. Department of Justice, Office of Community Oriented Policing Services, 2009), http://ric-zai-inc.com/ric.php?page=detail&id=COPS-P172.

6. "The SARA Model," Center for Problem-Oriented Policing, 2013, www.popcenter.org/about/?p=sara.

7. Ibid.

8. Ibid.

9. Ibid.

Successful Strategies: Alcohol and Substance Abuse

Pueblo of Isleta

About the Tribe

Centrally located in the Rio Grande Valley, the Pueblo of Isleta is 15 miles south of Albuquerque, New Mexico. The pueblo covers more than 329 square miles and has a diverse geographical terrain that ranges from forests in the Manzano Mountains in the east to the desert mesas of the Río Puerco in the west.[10] The government of the Pueblo of Isleta was formed in the 1930s, and the pueblo is home to 3,980 enrolled members with a total population of 4,853. The Isleta Police Department is a 638 self-governing Bureau of Indian Affairs contract agency.

The name Isleta is Spanish for "little island."[11] Many "traditions, songs and dances are still practiced and passed down from generation to generation."[12] The historic St. Augustine Church, rebuilt in 1716, is located on the pueblo's main plaza.[13]

Website: www.isletapueblo.com

Overview

The Isleta Pueblo hosted the Tribal Resources Grant Program's (TRGP) Tribal Community and Police Problem-Solving Teams (TTEAMS) training on October 21–22, 2009. Attendees from Isleta Pueblo represented law enforcement, natural resources, behavioral health, and a community business. In addition, representatives from the Jicarilla Apache Nation public safety and health and human services; the Mescalero Apache Tribe resort and casino security; and Pueblo of Sandia law enforcement attended the training. The TTEAMS training afforded some departments the opportunity to meet and confer for the first time, where they

▲ *The annual Isleta Pueblo community parade, organized collaboratively between the Isleta Police Department and Isleta Social Services Department, is held in conjunction with National Child Abuse Prevention Month in April, and the floats contain child protection messages.*

learned they all were confronting common problems. These departments had been unaware of the others' efforts to address the most common concern of substance abuse, specifically methamphetamine and prescription drugs. According to the Isleta Police Department's chief of police, Kevin Mariano, about 85 to 90 percent of all reported crimes were estimated to be related directly to substance abuse.

Strategy to Address Substance Abuse

As a result of the TTEAMS training, the tribe adopted a comprehensive approach using partnerships to address critical issues, including substance abuse, affecting the tribe. The approach encompasses the following strategies:

1. **Improve internal and interagency communication.**
    a. Identify key individuals to develop communication strategies.
    b. Hold regular meetings to develop communication strategies.
    c. Implement communication strategies.

10. Veronica E. Velarde Tiller, *Tiller's Guide to Indian Country* (Albuquerque, NM: Bow Arrow Publishing Company, 2005).
11. "Welcome to the Pueblo of Isleta, New Mexico," Pueblo of Isleta, 2013, www.isletapueblo.com.
12. "New Mexico Legends: Ancient History Beyond Albuquerque," Legends of America, 2010, www.legendsofamerica.com/nm-isleta.html.
13. Ibid.

2. **Focus on teamwork and inclusiveness.**

   a. Identify key stakeholders/agencies to enhance and encourage teamwork with the other agencies.

   b. Hold the initial meeting.

      i. Identify how each individual agency is addressing the substance abuse issue, and discuss challenges and successes to date.

      ii. Identify each agency's resources and areas where resources can be shared.

      iii. Develop common goals and a common vision for the community and approaches to address the issue.

      iv. Identify team leader(s) to keep momentum going and communication open.

   c. Schedule regular meetings, and set meeting agendas prior to each meeting.

3. **Create and implement narcotics/gang task force officer positions.**

   a. Obtain support and buy-in from the tribal council.

   b. Identify funding.

   c. Define job descriptions and responsibilities.

   d. Post positions.

   e. Interview candidates.

   f. Hire and train officers.

   g. Share task force information with other agencies in the community.

4. **Raise community awareness about prescription drug abuse.**

   a. Identify target audience(s) for awareness campaign, and develop prevention messages geared toward specific audiences such as parents, teens, elders, etc.

   b. Develop a partnership with a local tribal clinic to address and monitor prescription usage and refills.

   c. Identify safe drop-off site(s) for prescription drugs.

   d. Post information about safe medicine disposal throughout the community, such as in health care provider offices, pharmacies, etc.

   e. Provide training for law enforcement on how to recognize individuals under the influence of prescription drugs and signs of abuse.

5. **Host a youth conference.**

   a. Develop a planning committee/advisory board.

   b. Identify the target audience/age group.

   c. Outline goals/objectives of the conference.

   d. Identify the conference theme.

   e. Solicit any donations or sponsorship necessary to run the event.

   f. Develop the conference agenda, and invite presenters.

   g. Plan any special events to be included.

   h. Advertise the conference to the community, schools, parents, youth, etc.

Outcomes to Date

1. **Improve internal and interagency communication.**

   The Isleta Police Department has adopted more open, internal communication that promotes full disclosure of information. Department staff—e.g., communications, records, investigations, and data analysts—have come together to review and update policies and procedures. Ten new chapters were added to the current policy, and the revised policy was sent to the tribe's Legal Department for review.

In addition, the tribal government building complex was recently consolidated by placing the tribal court, appellate court, and tribal police in the same building, which now allows enhanced interdepartmental interaction and face-to- face meetings.

Because of enhanced interdepartmental collaboration and communication, law enforcement and court judges identified the need to develop a wellness court. To accomplish this, law enforcement and court judges set plans into motion to find a coordinator who will be committed to developing the wellness court.

2. **Focus on teamwork and inclusiveness.**

The Isleta Police Department discovered that various Isleta Pueblo departments and programs were offering a fragmented approach to address substance abuse. This often caused conflicts and miscommunication. In order to resolve the issue, the departments started to work together to share resources and provide the community with consistent information. A multidisciplinary team was developed that includes representatives from social services, behavioral health, tribal courts, truancy, and law enforcement. The team meets on a weekly basis to discuss resources and ideas to address community safety issues including alcohol and substance abuse, truancy, and any other issues occurring in the community.

3. **Create and implement narcotics/gang task force officer positions.**

The Isleta Police Department worked with the tribal governor to gain support to create two narcotics/gang task force officer positions and succeeded. In 2010, the police department hired two officers to fill this role. Law enforcement coordinated resources among other departments, including social services, schools, the health department, and government officials, to identify drug dealers and possible gang members on the reservation. The tribal police department worked collaboratively with agencies outside of the reservation and with other drug task force units in New Mexico.

One of the officers also serves as a school resource officer (SRO) and works closely with youths in the school system and at community events and school sporting events. This helped build relationships and more trust with community members and youths. The SRO also conducted an active shooter drill at the school.

In 2012, the tribe reported a dramatic drop in tagging/graffiti incidents because the narcotics/gang task force officers were able to identify the individuals responsible for committing vandalism. The offenders were adjudicated and worked with the officers to paint over the graffiti.

4. **Raise community awareness about prescription drug abuse.**

The community reported a problem about tribal members using others' prescription medicines. Kids also were stealing their parents' or other family members' prescriptions. The community directed its efforts to raise awareness and provide educational opportunities about the dangers of prescription drug abuse. Law enforcement distributed brochures and pamphlets throughout the community and shared information on how legitimate users of prescription drugs can safeguard these items from others and how they can safely dispose unused prescription medication. In addition, the police department's school resource officer is working to set up a prescription drug drop-off site.

The police department will soon be hosting an open house where it will also distribute information on prescription drug abuse.

5. **Host a youth conference.**

In the summer, the community holds an annual youth conference typically at the community recreation center. Youth attending the conference are grouped by age to participate in activities.

The 2011 conference, attended by more than 200 youths, focused on bullying, gang issues, and substance abuse. The events included a poster contest with the top 10 winners receiving prizes. Local agencies provided speakers to present on a variety of topics.

The 2012 all-day conference was held at the local school for 135 children in first through sixth grades and focused on gang awareness and gun safety. School administration strongly supported this initiative; in place of regular classes, students attended presentations. For the summer of 2013, the community plans to reverse the typical pattern of presentations—tribal youths will present issues that they confront in the community.

Lessons Learned

First, community members needed to know how to report crimes and suspicious activities and what type of information to include in their reporting: e.g., a description of the subject along with the time and place of activity.

It was beneficial to have new officers participate in a formal, four-hour, cultural indoctrination class to better understand the specific customs and traditions of community members.

Additional Community Policing Activities

- On May 25, 2012, Isleta Pueblo held a Missing Children's Day event that focused on Internet safety tips, law enforcement training, an explanation of technology-assisted crimes against children, and training for first responders and tribal officials to help recognize signs of danger and exploitation of children. Although the tribe does not have a problem with runaways, it wants to be proactive in addressing youths' exposure to potential online dangers such as predators and Internet crimes.

- One interesting tradition is that the tribe passes down a tribal position—i.e., traditional sheriff—to one of its members who "inherits" the position. The traditional sheriff's job is to respond to the death of a tribal member and to ensure that the deceased is spiritually and culturally sent on his or her journey in accordance with ancient tribal customs. In past times, there was a disconnect between the traditional sheriff and nontribal law enforcement, which felt that the traditional sheriff was interfering with nontribal law enforcement's death investigations. A change in nontribal law enforcement personnel prompted the creation of a tribal liaison position to help repair relationships between the tribe's traditional sheriff and the nontribal law enforcement community. The liaison officer now works with the traditional sheriff to ensure not only that the needs of tribal customs and tradition are met but also that nontribal law enforcement still is able to investigate deaths and other crimes properly. The nontribal liaison officer also works with the elders and cultural leaders to explain the actions of the police department in the hope of increasing cooperation and gaining acceptance.

- The tribal community hosts a law enforcement day each year. The most recent one was held in May 2012 with an open house of the tribal government complex. The event included various awards and recognitions. Participants included regional tribal agencies, adjacent law enforcement agencies, and the community. The event sent a message that different agencies and groups are willing to coordinate their efforts to keep the public safe.

- The Isleta Police Department uses Indian Highway Safety Program funding to maintain an active traffic division. The department uses a team approach to address specific traffic-related matters such as proper signage, engineering for tribal roads, and accident hot spots in an effort to reduce the number of accidents within the community.

- Every April, Isleta Social Services Department, in collaboration with the Isleta Police Department, organizes a community parade held in conjunction with the National Child Abuse Prevention Month. A week before the parade, representatives from law enforcement, the fire department, and other tribal agencies hold a popular meet-and-greet event. The parade itself includes floats with child protection messages and candy handed out to the youths. A reception follows, featuring hamburgers from meat donated by a local ranch. This event continues to be very popular with the community.

- On-duty officers are directed to spend time reading at the local elementary school 10 to 15 minutes per week. Their presence has helped them befriend these young, impressionable children and shows the officers in a different light.

- The pueblo's Behavioral Health Department organizes a yearly "Walk the Path," a 1.5-mile long march that is lit with luminaries memorializing those who died traumatically as a result of violence, suicide, or an accident. The march also recognizes the impact such incidents have on surviving family and friends.

Contact Information

Isleta Police Department
Tribal Road 61, Building 10
Isleta, NM 87022
Ph: 505-869-9711 (office)
Fax: 505-869-2407

Lead Contact

Kevin Mariano, Chief of Police | poi06001@isletapueblo.com

Lead Agency Demographics

The Isleta Police Department has 30 sworn positions, which include three traffic enforcement officers, one detective, and one gang and drug investigator. An additional civilian staff of 12 includes six dispatchers and their supervisor, two records clerks, a special project administrator, a secretary, and an assistant secretary.

Mission Statement

"The mission of the Isleta Police Department is to serve and protect the Pueblo of Isleta; uphold the laws and ordinances established by the Tribe, Federal, and the State of New Mexico; foster an atmosphere of mutual respect for citizens; render service in a professional manner; utilize the public safety and leadership skills that serve to guide and protect us in the daily demands of our jobs as Law Enforcement Officers."[14]

. . . .

14. Isleta Police Department, "Mission Statement" (paper presented to Fox Valley Technical College, Appleton, WI, February 21, 2013).

Leech Lake Band of Ojibwe

About the Tribe

The Leech Lake Band of Ojibwe covers 1,050 square miles and encompasses four counties in Minnesota. Tribal headquarters is located in Cass Lake, and there are 11,000 enrolled members, 4,100 of whom live on the reservation. The total population (tribal members and nontribal members) living on the reservation is more than 10,000.[15] In addition to the Cass Lake community, there are 16 other communities—13 on the reservation and three off the reservation.

Website: www.llojibwe.com

Overview

The Leech Lake Band of Ojibwe hosted the TTEAMS training on June 23–24, 2010. Attendees from the Leech Lake Band of Ojibwe included community members and representatives from a variety of tribal agencies and disciplines, including law enforcement, behavioral health/treatment, ambulance service, gaming, tribal development, family violence program, human resources, regulatory board, and education. Representatives from the Red Lake Nation Tribal Courts and Pike Bay Police Department also attended the training. The Leech Lake Tribal Police Department's initial intent in hosting the training was to build community trust. During the training, attendees identified that substance abuse was severely impacting the community, and prescription drug abuse was on the rise.

Strategy to Address Substance Abuse

The community wanted a proactive response to address the issue of substance abuse systematically. They took a unique approach and adopted a public health response that included doing the following:

1. **Declare a public health emergency.**
   a. Identify circumstances that would warrant a public health emergency.
   b. Identify confidentiality laws and privacy rules.
   c. Identify a strategy to declare the emergency through the following:
      i.   Media
      ii. Social networking sites
      iii. Public announcements
   d. Work with partners to define roles in communicating the message.

2. **Form a Public Health Emergency Response Team.**
   a. Identify and invite key stakeholders to become part of the team.
   b. Identify goals and objectives.
   c. Plan the initial meeting, and set a regular meeting schedule.

3. **Hire a meth coordinator to assist the Leech Lake Tribal Police Department.**
   a. Define the role and responsibilities of the coordinator position.
   b. Post job application information.
   c. Select and hire a coordinator.
   d. Provide the coordinator with appropriate training.

. . . .
15. "Demographics," Leech Lake Band of Ojibwe, 2013, www.llojibwe.com.

Outcomes to Date

1. **Declare a public health emergency.**

   On April 1, 2011, the tribal council declared a public health emergency to address prescription drug abuse. The council sent the declaration first to tribal government employees through a letter. Then the council passed a tribal resolution, and the tribal newspaper published the information.

2. **Form a Public Health Emergency Response Team.**

   The tribal council formed a Public Health Emergency Response Team (PHERT), which included law enforcement, Indian Health Services, social services, and Leech Lake Child Welfare representatives. The PHERT coordinated a comprehensive, community-wide response to the epidemic, allowing other tribal agencies to be involved with training and public education for adults and youth.

   The Leech Lake Tribal Police Department organized a two-day training on prescription drug abuse in Indian Country in June 2012. The first day of training was open to tribal government, gaming representatives, and law enforcement; the second day was open to the community. Titles of training sessions included Drug Abuse Issues Affecting Indian Country, Types of Prescription Drugs Abused, Signs of Prescription Drug Abuse, Opioid Addiction and Heroin, Over-the-Counter Drugs, Drug Endangered Children: Signs and Symptoms, Effective Strategies and Techniques for Prevention, and Next-Step Resources to Respond Today.

   A panel presentation provided an opportunity for gaming representatives, tribal government, and community members to ask general questions about prescription drug abuse and consequences for dealing drugs. Panelists included representatives from tribal law enforcement; the Leech Lake Opiate Program; and the Cass Lake Indian Health Services, which explained its role in addressing prescription drug abuse and protocols for dispersing information.

   PHERT also conducted a survey in the tribal community and surrounding communities relying on three of the 14 on-reservation local Indian councils. The survey asked the community about information and solutions pertaining to public health issues and was initially distributed to individuals and then later in a group setting. Survey results identified potential solutions including additional educational opportunities, awareness campaigns, and stricter enforcement and sentencing for illegal activity to address these drug abuse issues.

3. **Hire a meth coordinator to assist the Leech Lake Tribal Police Department.**

   The Leech Lake Tribal Police Department selected a methamphetamine coordinator to organize community outreach and drug awareness efforts. For example, the police department provides meth and drug training for the schools, for gaming employees, and at tribal employee orientation. Also, the department publicized its awareness efforts by creating a billboard on U.S. Highway 2 that read, "Don't Meth with Me. I'm Drug Free."

   The meth coordinator and substance abuse program coordinator continue to provide education and raise awareness about the dangers of meth and other drug trends such as K2, spice, and bath salts. The meth coordinator works with the tribal schools, public schools, the alternative school, Leech Lake Child Welfare, and tribal council to provide approximately two presentations per week.

   Since implementing community policing activities, the tribal police department has collected information, including data in the Unified Crime Report (UCR), suggesting that alcohol and substance abuse-related crime has decreased. Twenty-four gang members are facing federal indictments for their criminal actions.

Because of the indictments, the number of search warrants for suspected crack houses has decreased an estimated 70 percent, and search warrants for other drugs have decreased 40 percent.

Lessons Learned

To be successful in community policing efforts, the tribal police department stressed that the police must build trust and rapport with the community.

Additional Community Policing Activities

The Leech Lake Tribal Police Department has participated in community activities, including National Night Out, a crime prevention/neighborhood organizational event; school kickoff events; and local pow-wows.

A second public safety issue that had been identified during the TTEAMS training was an increase in the number of burglaries and home invasions. The tribal police department is implementing additional community policing activities to deter crime, such as increased patrol and making more contacts with community members to develop a more proactive response.

▲ *The Leech Lake Tribal Police Department hosted Prescription Drug Abuse in Indian Country training in June 2012.*

Contact Information

Leech Lake Tribal Police Department
6530 US Highway 2 NW
Cass Lake, MN 56633
Ph: 218-335-8277
Fax: 218-335-8294

Lead Contact

Kenneth Washington, Assistant Chief of Police | kenneth.washington@llpolice.org

Lead Agency Demographics

The Leech Lake Tribal Police Department was formed in 1999 under the state of Minnesota's civil regulatory authority. The department has 22 officers, including two school resource officers, two domestic violence investigators, and an investigator assigned to methamphetamine investigations and narcotic pill diversions.

The department also has eight dispatchers; three support staff; one community service officer; and three special project coordinators of which one is assigned as a substance abuse coordinator, one is the methamphetamine coordinator, and one acts as a transcriptionist.

Mission Statement

"The Leech Lake Band of Ojibwe Tribal Police Department is committed to a Loyal Partnership of Public Service, the prevention of crime and the preservation of the peace, safety, and order within the Leech Lake Reservation.

We are committed to fostering an atmosphere of mutual respect with all citizens' civil liberties who we make contact by rendering service in a professional and courteous manner.

Instill Officer dedication and pride by maintaining a quality work environment, along with effective training and leadership that will result in community based policing.

We will provide the citizens of the Leech Lake Reservation a safe, crime free environment and promote positive family growth through effective law enforcement and community education."[16]

. . . .

16   Leech Lake Band of Ojibwe Tribal Police Department, "Mission Statement" (presented to Fox Valley Technical College, Appleton, WI, February 19, 2013).

Aleut Community of St. Paul Island

About the Tribe

St. Paul Island is located in the Bering Sea between Russia and the Alaskan mainland. The island, formed by volcanic eruptions, covers 44 square miles and is made up of cinder cones, sandy beaches, and sea cliffs.[17] St. Paul Island has 474 inhabitants, 85 percent of whom are Alaskan Natives. In the late 1700s, Russian fur traders discovered the island, as well as surrounding islands, and as a result traditional Russian Orthodox values and believes remain strong.[18]

Facebook: www.facebook.com/St.PaulIsland

Overview

The tribal community hosted the TTEAMS training on August 16–17, 2011. Attendees from St. Paul Island included representatives from its law enforcement, behavioral health, the domestic violence and sexual assault program, health and human services, and the court.

Although the tribe is a "damp" community where beer is allowed, the possession or selling of hard liquor is banned, and consequently, a single bottle of liquor can sell for more than $100. This situation was cause for concern, and during the training the tribal community identified alcohol and substance abuse and associated social disorder as its major concerns.

Strategy to Address Alcohol and Substance Abuse

1. **Develop a juvenile risk-reduction program.**
   a. Identify the target audience and age group.
   b. Invite subject-matter experts to develop the curriculum.
   c. Identify ways to incorporate traditional and cultural values.
   d. Identify ways to gain community buy-in for the program.

2. **Provide educational programs for adults.**
   a. Utilize developed programs for youths, and make necessary curriculum updates relevant to adults.
   b. Identify dates and locations to host the program.
   c. Outline a request process for the program to be offered on an as-needed basis.

3. **Provide educational programs at the school.**
   a. Meet with the school to plan specific dates and time to host the Drug Abuse Resistance and Education (DARE) program.
   b. Identify a lead officer or person to run the program.
   c. Distribute information to all teachers, students, and parents.

4. **Sponsor a wellness gathering.**
   a. Hold advisory board meeting to focus specifically on planning the event.
   b. Identify the target audience.
   c. Select dates, and coordinate a schedule with the host facility.
   d. Plan agenda and activities.
   e. Invite presenters/speakers.
   f. Solicit any donations if necessary.
   g. Promote event in the community once it is scheduled.

. . . .
17. Velarde Tiller, *Tiller's Guide to Indian Country*, 234.
18. Ibid.

Outcomes to Date

1. Develop a juvenile risk-reduction program.

The Department of Community Safety and Peace sponsors a juvenile risk-reduction program titled "Prime for Life," which is designed for youths from 13 to 21 years of age and focuses on making healthy choices. The Alaska State Court system originally developed this 12-hour course for first- and second-time offenders required to attend an alcohol/drug education class. The Aleut Community of St. Paul Island adapted the course to incorporate Aleut values and traditions to educate and inform youth about the negative impact of alcohol and substance abuse, and these values are included in the "Protecting What I Value" section of the curriculum.

A roundtable discussion on the unique island geography (regional and local), wildlife, culture, language, and family life provides youths with an opportunity to acknowledge and appreciate the uniqueness of their heritage. The program currently has one certified instructor, and the tribe plans to train and certify more.

The curriculum for the program includes the following topics:
- Impairment problems
- Health problems
- Biology
- Choices in life
- Psychological influences
- Social influences
- Definition of a standard drink
- High/low tolerance
- Quantity vs. frequency
- Building low-risk guidelines (learning the 1-2-3 rule)
- Phases of use: Phase 1, Phase 2, Phase 3, Phase 4
- State-dependent learning
- Other drugs and impairment
- Self-assessment
- Protecting what I value

Activities in the program include the following:
- Pros and cons
- Thinking about my future—choices and outcomes
- My formula—social support and my relationship to others
- Support inside myself
- My commitment
- Be ready, be quick
- My letter (which every participant writes to himself/herself or a loved one and the instructor mails three months after the program ends)

2. Provide educational programs for adults.

An adult program, similar to the youth program, is based on the Alcohol/Drug Information School (ADIS) and is intended for first-time DUI offenders or offenders with an alcohol-related domestic violence incident. The primary goal of ADIS is to reduce the number of alcohol- and drug-related crimes and to help individuals understand, change, or stop their high-risk substance abuse. Participants receive information on Alaska laws and penalties related to alcohol and/or other drugs; they explore how alcohol and/or other drugs affect their behavior, family, and community; they examine the differences between substance use, abuse, and addiction; and they develop a "change plan" to avoid future problems with alcohol and other drugs. Participants also receive a workbook that they complete during class. Its activities are designed to encourage the participants to apply information learned to their personal circumstances.

St. Paul Island's ADIS program meets the requirements of both the Alaska State judicial system and the tribal court system. The course is offered as needed, and the course can accommodate up to 10 participants at a time based on available facility space. The program is open to the general public, including individuals referred by their employers or parents concerned about their child's use and abuse of alcohol or drugs.

Future program plans include integrating a screening tool as opposed to a full assessment to determine whether individuals would be best served by this program. Those needing a full assessment would be referred to the Pribilof Island Health Center where participants would follow a designated treatment plan, either as an outpatient or as an inpatient resident at a treatment facility to work on transitioning back into the tribal community.

3. **Provide educational programs at the school.**

The Department of Community Safety and Peace assigns an officer to the local school to provide drug and alcohol abuse information through the DARE program. The officer collaborates with teachers to schedule the program and teaches the classes two grades at a time (fifth and sixth grades, and seventh and eighth grades), reaching approximately 20 students per year.

4. **Sponsor a wellness gathering.**

The tribe's Strategic Planning Advisory Board, comprised of representatives from the city, tribal government, tribal school, the health center, behavioral health, the fisherman's group, and youth and elder representatives, will sponsor a wellness gathering in the spring of 2013. Breakout sessions will include a variety of topics, including healthy lifestyles, historical trauma, juvenile delinquency prevention, parenting, healthy families, teen dating violence, education and employment, obesity prevention, and tobacco prevention/education. The Board's goal is to present quarterly follow-up events that focus on sobriety and the well-being of community members.

In 2013, the Department of Community Safety and Peace will analyze the impact of these programs. Based on information gathered to date, there are strong indicators that these programs are having a positive impact in the community.

Lessons Learned

To be effective, people need to come together to share their same concerns and come up with solutions. Phil Zavadil, director of the Department of Community Safety and Peace, states that when addressing community policing issues, "everybody has something to offer."

Additional Community Policing Activities

The Department of Community Safety and Peace established a memorandum of understanding (MOU) with the adjoining local, non-Native police department. The MOU may need to undergo revisions because there is a new police chief and staff at the local police department.

The department has a designated school resource officer (SRO) who interacts with 80 children in the local school from kindergarten through 12th grade. The department plans to develop an MOU with the school to outline the responsibilities of the SRO and a process for sharing and exchanging information.

Contact Information

Aleut Community of St. Paul Island
Department of Community Safety and Peace
PO Box 86
St. Paul Island, AK 99680
Ph: 907-546-3200
Fax: 907-546-3254

Lead Contact

Phil Zavadil, Director | pazavadil@tgspi.com

Lead Agency Demographics

The department employs two full-time officers, supplemented by three part-time and seasonal officers and one civilian administrative clerk.

Mission Statement

The Department of Community Safety and Peace (DCSP) has identified the following mission:

"DCSP shall operate under the philosophy of community policing and restorative justice, and shall strive to achieve close interagency coordination between all law enforcement agencies exercising jurisdiction on St. Paul Island.

DCSP shall encourage cooperation of all residents of St. Paul Island to reduce and limit the opportunities for crime and violations of Federal, State, City, and Tribal law.

In an effort to encourage Community cooperation, DCSP shall provide regular opportunities for Community participation in enforcement education and Community feedback of law enforcement activities.

When implementing enforcement strategies and policies, DCSP shall consider the overall effect on tribal members and the Community and operate in a manner that minimizes any negative impact of enforcement activities.

DCSP shall implement all strategies, policies, and enforcement activities in a fair and impartial manner, consistent with the notions of justice.

Except where expressly provided otherwise in this Policy or applicable Federal Law, DCSP shall perform its duties and exercise its powers in a manner consistent with Tribal ordinances, policies, and unwritten customary laws."[19]

. . . .

19. Department of Community Safety and Peace, "Management Philosophy" (presented to Fox Valley Technical College, Appleton, WI, July 16, 2013).

Tonkawa Tribe of Oklahoma

About the Tribe

The Tonkawa Tribe of Oklahoma is located in Kay County, approximately 100 miles north of Oklahoma City.[20] The tribe covers more than 1,232 acres comprising 994 acres of federal trust land and 238 acres of individual allotments. The name Tonkawa, or Tickanwatic, means "real people," and the Wichita name for the Tonkawa people is Tonkaweya, which means "they all stay together."[21] Presently, more than 500 people reside on Tonkawa land, 481 of whom are enrolled members.

Website: www.tonkawatribe.com

Overview

The Tonkawa tribal community hosted the TTEAMS training on October 18–19, 2010. Attendees from the Tonkawa Tribe of Oklahoma included representatives from its law enforcement, tribal administration, grants management, housing, substance abuse program, and social services. In addition, representatives from Otoe-Missouria Tribe youth leadership and language programs and Kaw Nation law enforcement attended. Collectively, the group identified domestic violence linked with alcohol abuse as key issues in the community.

Strategy to Address Domestic Violence and Alcohol Abuse

The Tonkawa Tribe of Oklahoma and Fort Oakland Police Department acknowledge that a key component to address and respond to domestic violence and alcohol abuse is to understand that a problem cannot be eliminated unless the underlying causes are identified.

With this philosophy, the officer looks at all the behaviors of the individual and devises a permanent solution to the issues rather than incarcerating him or her.

The tribe and police department identified the following strategies to achieve their ultimate goal of providing alternatives to incarceration:

1. **Create and implement a court review board.**
    a. Invite key stakeholders to meet and discuss the development of the court review board.
    b. Outline the board member selection process.
    c. Develop a vision and mission statement.
    d. Identify goals and objectives.
    e. Define roles and responsibilities of board members and assign roles and tasks as appropriate.
    f. Set quarterly meeting schedules and agenda.

2. **Deter juvenile crime.**
    a. Work with other service providers to identify potential underlying causes.
    b. Develop programs to foster more relationships between police and youths, and incorporate cultural elements into the programs where applicable.

3. **Enhance social services.**
    a. Evaluate available services.
    b. Identify gaps in service and opportunities for improvement.
    c. Identify ways to collaborate with all service providers.
    d. Define guidelines and terms for offenders who would be good candidates for alternative sentencing options.
    e. Provide updated information to the community about available services.

. . . .

20 "Tonkawa Tribal Profile," The Tonkawa Tribe of Oklahoma, 2013, www.tonkawatribe.com/profile/profile.htm.

21 Ibid.

4. **Create and implement a community policing officer position.**

   a. Identify available or obtain new funding for the position.

   b. Define job roles, responsibilities, and desired outcomes.

   c. Post job application information.

   d. Interview candidates.

   e. Select, hire, and train the officer.

   f. Schedule regular meetings with the community policing officer to discuss progress and needs or issues identified by the community.

5. **Create and implement a community sentence officer position.**

   a. Schedule a meeting between the tribal court and Fort Oakland Police Department, as well as other service providers as appropriate, to discuss the desired roles and responsibilities of the position and desired outcomes.

   b. Outline job description, and post position.

   c. Interview candidates.

   d. Select and hire officer.

   e. Provide appropriate training so that the officer is up to date on tribal probation and alternative sentencing options, such as electronic monitoring, community service, work release programs, etc.

Outcomes to Date
___

1. **Implement a court review board.**

   Members of the board include representatives from tribal court, the police department, prosecution, victim advocacy, housing, child welfare, and social services. They meet quarterly to review recent criminal cases with the aim of identifying trends and locations that need more specific attention and/or enforcement. The board made note of trends, including graffiti, vandalism, and radio thefts frequently committed by youths and recidivism among adult offenders.

   By working closely with the tribe's social services and Indian Child Welfare Office as well as the Bureau of Indian Affairs (BIA), the board aims to identify and address underlying causes of criminal behavior such as unsupervised youths or those who have substance abuse issues. Since the implementation of the board, the tribe reported a decline in substance abuse issues. However, domestic violence reports have increased. Also, both law enforcement and the tribal court have noticed that victims have become more comfortable making reports to law enforcement. Fort Oakland police believe this would not be the case without trust and rapport built through community outreach programs.

2. **Deter juvenile crime.**

   The tribe identified that alcohol and substance abuse and domestic violence issues resulted in the high rate of juvenile crime in the community. The tribe also noticed that a high volume of juveniles were involved in graffiti, break-ins, petty thefts, shoplifting, and drug use. Parents or other family members who commit acts of domestic violence or engage in drug/alcohol abuse influence youth behavior, making the youths more likely to continue the cycle of violence. The youths most likely to be involved in delinquent behaviors are those in middle school (seventh, eighth, and ninth graders) because they feel their parents' and family's behaviors are normal and, as a result, they begin to act the same way.

   Like many tribal authorities, the tribe currently does not have detention services for most of these youths. As an alternative to incarceration, Fort Oakland officers wanted to deter crime among youth through increased monitoring and interaction with all youths.

A tribal youth program, under the tribe's Johnson O'Malley (JOM) Program, offers youths transportation to events such as the Oklahoma City Thunder basketball games. The JOM program also sponsored tribal youths who wanted to participate in the state spelling bee. Furthermore, it offers after-school programs and activities; however, before students can participate in the activities, they must complete their schoolwork and homework. JOM program tutors are available to assist struggling students with their assignments. JOM program staff serves as positive role models for the youths, and Fort Oakland officers stop by to visit and interact with the youths and participate in program activities. The tribe also has plans to develop additional youth programs.

Cultural components also are being incorporated into these programs to address juvenile crime. A tribal representative holds sweat lodges every Wednesday and Sunday for youths and adults. The youths not only have been actively participating in the sweat lodges but also are attending Tonkawa language classes and traditional handball games. Through these activities, youths have the opportunity to interact with positive role models.

3. **Enhance social services.**

    The tribe offered additional services through the court to treat community members with alcohol and drug abuse issues. These services include alcohol and substance abuse rehabilitation programs, counseling, working with the Court Review Board, and participating in the tribal youth program as mentioned above.

    The court also offers offenders either diversion or suspended sentences if they go through a series of counseling sessions and other related services. The tribe also collaborates with the Bureau of Indian Affairs–Pawnee Agency, which also assists in providing appropriate services for those involved in domestic violence incidents and those who have alcohol and substance abuse issues.

4. **Create and implement a community policing officer position.**

    Both elders and youths are greatly impacted by domestic violence and alcohol and substance abuse issues in the community. In addition, there is a significant amount of elder abuse; children and taking advantage of their elders for money and prescription drugs. Youths witness repeated incidents of domestic violence and alcohol and drug abuse in their homes. In response to these issues, the Fort Oakland Police Department created a position for a new community policing officer who works specifically with the elders and youths, coordinating activities for both groups and serving as a point of contact when issues arise.

    Because this position is new, the community policing officer is in the process of building trust and rapport with the elders and youths. Both groups are beginning to accept the officer and speak with him about issues they are experiencing. The officer helps these individuals locate appropriate services as needed. The police department completes case reports and works with the Bureau of Indian Affairs to conduct investigations as needed.

    The community policing officer is more involved with the schools and follows up on truancy cases through "home" visits with kids and families. During these visits, the officer identifies any concerns of neglect, abuse, or other crime. In one case, a grandmother who was raising a youth had to be hospitalized. During a home visit, the officer found the youth at home alone with no adult supervision. The community policing officer and the department worked with the tribe's Indian Child Welfare Office to notify other family members to get the appropriate help for the neglected youth. The department plans to continue enhancing the officer's role in the schools.

The community policing officer also meets regularly with other service providers such as housing and the court.

5. **Create and implement a community sentence officer position.**

   The community sentence officer who works through the tribal court serves as a probation officer, a compliance monitor, and a pre-sentence officer. As compliance monitor, the officer ensures the offender completes all court-mandated requirements, including drug tests; he conducts home visits; and he calls or visits employers to make sure the offender maintains his or her job. The officer also ensures the offender participates in court-ordered programs, such as Alcoholics Anonymous or the Domestic Violence Batterers' program. Prior to the offender being incarcerated, the officer, who also serves as a probation officer, works with the offender and the family to address family issues. This may include the officer checking in with the offender, connecting the offender with needed resources or services, or reporting status updates to the judge. The community sentence officer also works with the police and other service providers to share information, identify community needs, and provide updates on community members.

   The Fort Oakland Police Department reported a 50 percent increase in the number of domestic violence contacts (arrests or other events that bring people into the court system). The department believes the increased reporting is a result of community outreach efforts and the enhanced collaboration between service providers to address the issue.

   Because they adopted a community policing philosophy, and because they are more visible and approachable, officers are noticing a higher level of community involvement and trust. Tribal members are more apt to report concerns or problems. In addition, some members undergoing treatment are now recommending the same treatment protocol to others who might benefit.

Lessons Learned

The Fort Oakland Police Department's chief of police will continue efforts to establish a community board to help guide community policing activities. Domestic violence and alcohol abuse have deep rooted causes and will not be solved overnight or through an arrest.

Additional Community Policing Activities

Not many tribal members have a driver's license because either they've lost it due to alcohol or drug issues or they have not taken a driver's education class. Unfortunately, driver's education is offered only in the summer, and the cost, which must be paid up front, is too prohibitive for many families; thus, many youths are not able to go through the program and obtain their license. Future plans for the community policing officer include earning Driver's Education Instructor Certification so that he is able to train elders and youths.

The police department also engages youths in cultural events such as teaching traditional farming methods and cutting hay; camping where youths learn how to trail, hunt, and fish; and making bows and drums.

Contact Information
_____

Fort Oakland Police Department
1 Rush Buffalo Road
Tonkawa, OK 74653
Ph: 580-628-2340
Fax: 580-628-2337
Website: www.tonkawatribe.com/police.htm
Facebook page: https://www.facebook.com/pages/Fort-Oakland-Police-Department

Lead Contacts
_____

John Cooper, Chief of Police | JCooper@tonkawatribe.com

Marilyn Epley, Executive Planner | MEpley@tonkawatribe.com

Lead Agency Demographics
_____

The Fort Oakland Police Department has six sworn positions and five civilian positions, and the department recently hired a community policing officer.

Mission Statement

"The mission of the Fort Oakland Police Department is to continually strive to increase the standard of living of the citizens of Fort Oakland and the members of the Tonkawa Tribe through impartial police services designed to prevent, deter, and aggressively investigate criminal violations of the law."[22]

....

22. Fort Oakland Police Department, "Mission Statement" (presented to Fox Valley Technical College, Appleton, WI, July 25, 2013).

▲ The Leech Lake Tribal Police
Department publicized its meth
awareness campaign by creating
a billboard on U.S. Highway 2,
which runs through the reservation.

Lac du Flambeau Band of Lake Superior Chippewa

About the Tribe

Treaties established the Lac du Flambeau reservation in 1837 and 1842.[23] The tribal lands overlay two counties (Vilas and Oneida) in Wisconsin, covering 144 square miles. The reservation has 260 lakes; 65 miles of streams, rivers, and lakes; and 24,000 acres of wetlands. While tribal membership exceeds 3,000, the actual population of the reservation is 3,800, and that number increases to more than 50,000 during the summer because of the area's rich heritage and scenic location.

The band's name, Lac du Flambeau, means "Lake of the Torches" and refers to the practices of harvesting fish at night by torchlight.[24]

Website: www.ldftribe.com

Overview

The tribe hosted the TTEAMS training on April 6–8, 2009. Attendees from Lac du Flambeau Band of Lake Superior Chippewa included representatives from its tribal programs, courts, law enforcement department, domestic violence programs, victims' services, and health services. In addition, representatives from the Vilas County and Oneida County Sheriff's Departments were in attendance.

As a result of the training, the community identified gangs and related crimes as the main focus of their community policing efforts. The presence of gang members has become prevalent because of an increasing amount of drugs and money being exchanged in the community. Three active gangs received support from newly released prison inmates with ties to the tribal community.

Strategy to Address Gangs

Based on the TTEAMS Training, the attendees developed the following strategies to address their community's gang issues:

1. **Develop an intervention program.**
   a. Reach out to tribal agencies and key stakeholders interested in assisting with the development of the program.
   b. Hold meetings with school officials.
   c. Provide training for officers and school officials.
   d. Establish interagency law enforcement partnerships.

2. **Hire a gang specialist to work in the community.**
   a. Identify the role of the gang specialist.
   b. Select and hire a gang specialist.
   c. Identify potential funding sources and tribal agencies to support the gang specialist position.
   d. Create a schedule for the gang specialist to be present in the community to continually assess gang activity.

23. "About Us," Lac du Flambeau Band of Lake Superior Chippewa Indians, 2010, www.ldftribe.com/about_us.php.
24. Ibid.

3. **Address truancy and parental supervision issues.**
    a. Develop a formal relationship between schools and the Lac du Flambeau Tribal Police Department to address truancy.
        i. Assign officer(s) to assist school personnel with home visits.
        ii. Schedule home visits.
    b. Enforce a curfew.
        i. Select a curfew time and days for enforcement.
        ii. Define the enforcement policy, including curfew violations.
        iii. Disseminate curfew information to parents, the community, and schools.

4. **Provide alternative activities to deter youths from becoming involved in gangs and crime.**
    a. Identify and organize potential youth-related activities.
    b. Invite key stakeholders to assist in planning and implementing these activities.
    c. Identify and solicit any donations or supplies necessary for the activities.

5. **Implement a standardized dress code in schools.**
    a. Request price quotes from local vendors and select a uniform.
    b. Outline the policy including consequences for dress code violations.
    c. Distribute dress code and uniform purchasing information to parents and students.

6. **Remove graffiti.**
    a. Define a graffiti-reporting process (online and/or call-in information) and post reporting process information on tribal and police department websites.
    b. Seek donations of tools and products necessary to remove graffiti.
    c. Identify youths on supervision who will participate in graffiti removal as part of their community service.
    d. Assign adult supervisors, and recruit volunteers as needed.

7. **Increase police patrols.**
    a. Using the problem-oriented policing concept, identify specific areas or neighborhoods that require additional patrols.
    b. Assign officers to foot and bike patrol, and rotate shifts if necessary.

Outcomes to Date

1. **Develop an intervention program.**

    The Lac du Flambeau Tribal Police Department formed a Gang Resistance and Intervention Program (GRIP) to combat a growing gang problem. The tribe is working to inform the community, identify at-risk youths, and deter these youths from becoming involved in gangs.

    The GRIP task force meets monthly and comprises representatives from various Lac du Flambeau tribal programs including the Juvenile Justice Department, Indian Child Welfare Department, Education Center, the Family Resource Center, the Abinoojiiyag Center for youths, the cultural department, the Minobimaadiviiwin Coalition, and the community. In addition, school principals from both the local high school and grade school, as well as representatives from the Great Lakes Intertribal Council[25] and Vilas County Juvenile Justice, are on the task force.

. . . .

25. The Great Lakes Intertribal Council, Inc. (GLITC) is a consortium of 12 federally recognized Indian tribes in Wisconsin and Upper Michigan. The mission of the GLITC is to support member tribes in expanding self-determination efforts by providing services and assistance. GLITC uses a broad range of knowledge and experience to advocate for the improvement and unity of tribal governments, communities, and individuals. (See "Great Lakes Inter-Tribal Council, Inc.," www.glitc.org.)

The police department informed the community about GRIP by sending e-mails to tribal employees, distributing pamphlets, sending information to parents through the schools, and making phone calls.

If youths are truant or involved in gangs, the Juvenile Justice Department refers them to tribal court instead of being processed through state court. First-time offenders receive an alternative sentence and are mandated to attend an eight-hour gang-prevention training class with their parent(s). The tribe is currently preparing for the first class, which will consist of presentations by various tribal entities, including police department personnel, the judge, a dietician, juvenile justice staff, and Indian child welfare staff. Upon completing the class, youths will need to complete a community service project based on the offense and charge and must complete the project within a specific timeframe. In addition, both the youth and their parents will need to sign a behavioral agreement, and the tribal court may dismiss the charges after the youth completes the community service project.

The police department, courts, and GRIP program created a truancy and gang ordinance and presented it to the tribal council for approval (see Outcome to Date number 3 for additional information on truancy). The new gang ordinance defines what constitutes a gang member and criminal gang behavior and lists the penalties associated with criminal gang activity.

One of GRIP's goals is to provide wraparound services. The tribe's Juvenile Justice Department has a referral process in place for curfew violations, gang activity, and underage drinking. Juvenile justice works closely with the tribe's school resource officer (SRO) who conducts home visits based on referrals from juvenile justice. Referrals also come from school administrators, teachers, and directly to the Police Department. Family Resources, juvenile justice, and Indian child welfare provide additional services needed by the child or parent, such as parenting classes, as necessary.

2. **Hire a gang specialist to work in the community.**

    The community hired a gang specialist from Arizona with more than 27 years of law enforcement experience to come and work in the community 10 days a month. When working offsite, the specialist stays in contact with community members through e-mail and text messages. A partnership between the tribe and the public high school and grade school funds his services.

    The specialist focuses on community engagement and identification of gang activity. The specialist works closely with the GRIP task force and conducts regular assessments of what is occurring in the community and with the kids. The specialist then assists service providers to develop a plan based on current trends. The specialist also provides classes for school staff about gang signs and youth involvement in gangs and how parents and kids can talk to each other. In addition, the specialist holds a class called "Gang Proofing Your Child" that is extremely successful with parents.

3. **Address truancy and parental supervision issues.**

    The tribe recognized that a high truancy rate and poor parental supervision were related to youths becoming involved in gang activity. The police department, GRIP task force, and Healthy Community Action Team felt that acknowledging the gang presence and addressing their root issues would help to limit gang influence and thus reduce youths' participation in gang activities.

The SRO, in partnership with juvenile justice, leads talking circles at the high school that provide insight into underlying issues that could lead to truant behavior.

In an effort to reduce truancy, the school principal, accompanied by a police officer, personally visits truant children at their homes and encourages them to attend school. As a result of a collaborative effort among the courts, schools, law enforcement, and the gang specialist, a truancy ordinance was created by the police department, court, and GRIP Program and presented to the tribal council for approval. Prior to the ordinance, and according to the tribal constitution, parents could not be penalized for a truant child. There were very few measures to hold either the parent or truant child accountable. With the new ordinance, truancy is now considered a criminal offense.

Furthermore, parents are held responsible for truant behavior if a child is under the age of 14; consequences may include suspended access to tribal facilities and resources such as the bingo hall/casino, hunting, and fishing, etc. Any adult convicted of aiding a child's truancy also can be subject to serving time in an adult detention facility. Children over age 14 are held accountable for their delinquent behavior. Law enforcement now is able to enforce consequences that may include confiscating property such as gaming systems, cell phones, and computers. Items can be confiscated for a maximum of 90 days or until school attendance has improved.

The tribal president, chief of police, and a council member also have been making visits to the schools to discuss truancy and the importance of working hard in school and achieving good grades. These visits seem to have had an impact on the youths.

The tribe also enforced a curfew of 10:00 PM, seven days a week, for all youths under age 18. If a child repeatedly violates curfew, the police refer the offender to the GRIP program.

4. **Provide alternative activities to deter youth from becoming involved in gangs and crime.**

The police department plans regular activities and events to provide alternatives to gang involvement and delinquent behavior:

- **Ski and Tube:** In the summer, the department sponsors outings where youths can waterski or tube behind a boat. In support of this event, the chief of police donates the use of his personal boat. This promotes safe boating habits and allows for interactions between public safety staff, youths, their parents and grandparents, and community members. Approximately 150–200 people and all off-duty officers participate in this annual event. As part of the Ski and Tube outing, the domestic violence program, food pantry, and casino have pitched in to donate more than 300 burgers and brats, sports drinks, and water annually to help support the program. The community is extremely supportive of this summer activity.

- **Cops in the Gym:** During the winter, the department pays officers to spend time at the grade school to interact with youths and community members. This gives officers and staff the opportunity to meet and interact with tribal members, helping to reduce barriers in communication. The school resource officers also go to the youth center after school for an hour to participate with the youths in basketball, gym activities, and art projects.

- **Winter Games:** The tribe's cultural program hosts a week-long "Winter Games" event for youths that includes archery, spear throwing, and snow snake competition. On Friday, children from area grade schools are bussed in for the day's events that include cultural classes and storytelling. The main event, held on Saturday, includes a variety of activities, such as snowshoeing, cross-country skiing, skating, pond hockey, tubing, and a horse-drawn sleigh ride. Parents and community members are encouraged to participate in the activities.
- **Family Fun Days:** The Minobimaadiviiwin Coalition sponsors Family Fun Days several times throughout the winter months. The events include sledding and ice skating; coalition sponsors, local business, and various Lac du Flambeau programs provide food; and fundraisers offset costs.
- **Boxing Gym:** The police department uses the boxing gym in its basement as an opportunity to invite youths to become involved in boxing.

Oftentimes, youths fear law enforcement. However, opportunities such as these provide youths with an opportunity to interact with law enforcement, and as a result of the positive interaction, youths are beginning to feel more comfortable with law enforcement and are reporting gang or other crime-related information.

Furthermore, the two school resource officers are currently working on building a collaborative relationship with the youth center. Previously, a youth would be permanently banned from the youth center if he/she was involved in some kind of infraction. The school resource officers are working with the center's staff to help supervise the youths and identify alternative methods to permanent expulsion from the center.

Since the implementation of these programs, the police department noted an increase in reported abuse, suggesting that the youths are more comfortable talking with the police.

5. **Implement a standardized dress code in schools.**

In September 2011, the local K–8 school implemented a school uniform policy and prohibited the wearing of gang colors. The inexpensive school uniform comprises a collared polo-style shirt and blue jeans, which is both affordable for parents and stylish enough for the youths. As a result, even high school freshman are now less likely to wear gang indicia.

6. **Remove graffiti.**

The Neighborhood Watch Program, the housing department, and patrol officers assist in reporting graffiti found throughout the reservation and in housing areas to the school resource officer and the juvenile justice department that work with the youths to remove the graffiti as part of their community service. Under intense supervision by staff, youths promptly cover up or remove the graffiti with murals—the art teacher from the tribal youth center provides drawings for the murals. Since the implementation of this process, there has been noticeably less graffiti throughout the reservation.

7. **Increase police patrols.**

The police department arranged for bike and foot patrols that encourages more one-on-one interaction with community members and provides officers an opportunity to learn more about specific neighborhoods. Community members stop officers in the street to thank them for the increased patrols.

Since the implementation of this strategy, gang violence and gang presence decreased throughout the community. In addition, many youths disassociated themselves from the three local gangs. Other reported outcomes include decreased truancy, underage drinking, prescription drug abuse, and violent crime. Officers noted that community involvement and information sharing has significantly increased.

The success of these programs can be attributed to the support provided by the tribal president and tribal administration.

Lessons Learned

- A key element in the success of community policing programs, the school liaison program is extremely valuable in creating partnerships between law enforcement and school administrators and teachers to create a safe environment for learning and to promote information sharing and collaboration to solve social problems that students may face. By working hand in hand with social services, Indian child welfare, juvenile justice, school counselors, and teachers, the liaison program has been successful in curbing truancy, prescription drug abuse, and physical and sexual abuse, issues that can be related to the lack of parenting skills. The bond created between students and the officers has the potential for a long-term, positive impact. Maintaining this bond as well as creating new bonds with students is an ongoing process. Officers and students now recognize one another, and the connection between them is noticeable not just in school; the tribe has seen an improvement in the trust between members of the community and law enforcement when officers respond to calls for service in the home and in the public setting. Information sharing between school staff and law enforcement has increased because school officials now have another option for passing on information.

- Successful community policing efforts require collaboration and communication. For example, to combat issues such as truancy, all the different parties—school administrators, teachers, the school resource officer, etc.—need to become and remain connected with each other. Even though they are working in the school setting, each person has access to different information, and each has a different perspective, all of which needs to be shared.

- The success of community policing is related directly to engaging others to work together to find solutions to common issues. For example, the truancy program did not become successful or flourish until all the key stakeholders came together. In addition, when all stakeholders are involved, it is easier to identify key social issues occurring in the home. It also provides the group with the ability to place kids in a safe environment and work with the courts to change ordinances if necessary. According to Chief Brandenburg of the Lac du Flambeau Police Department, doing things differently is the key to being successful.

- Having buy-in and support from the tribal council, which is responsible for the administration of the whole community, is the key to successful programming.

- The tribe learned that using informal communication methods, such as word of mouth, to get information out to the community is important.

- Once goals are created, do not give up. Persistence is the key to accomplishing goals.

- Open communication is critical, and regularly scheduled meetings allow participating agencies to voice their opinions and concerns.

Additional Community Policing Activities

The tribal casino recently purchased a McGruff® costume for the police department, and it's used to stress safety and crime prevention within the community. The costume has promoted positive interactions with children at the tribal center and schools.

The police department covertly placed officers in retail liquor shops to discourage underage drinking. By implementing this "Cops in the Shops" process, youths never knew when officers would or would not be present at these stores.

The Minobimaadiviiwin Coalition hosts fundraisers to help run programs such as "Parents Who Host Lose the Most" and the "Prescription Drug Take-Back" program.

Several tribal organizations collaborate to host Lake Fest, which includes several events such as canoe races, water balloon tosses, and a dunk tank operated by the police department. Funds raised by this event go to assisting environmental programs and addressing community issues.

Contact Information

Lac du Flambeau Police Department
PO Box 337
Lac du Flambeau, WI 54538
Ph: 715-588-7717
Fax: 715-588-3461

Lakeland Union High School
9573 State Highway 70
Minocqua, WI 54548
Ph: 715-356-5252

Lac du Flambeau Elementary School
2899 Wisconsin 47
Lac du Flambeau, WI 54538
Ph: 715-588-3838

Lead Contacts

Robert Brandenburg, Chief of Police | echo262@frontiernet.net

Cecelia Stewart, Indian Education Mentor | stewart@luhs.k12.wi.us

Lead Agency Demographics

The police department has 14 sworn full-time officers, three part-time officers, two school resource officers, and one sexual assault investigator. It also employs three secretaries and four surveillance technicians who monitor strategically placed surveillance cameras throughout the community.

Mission Statement

"We, the members of Lac du Flambeau Tribal Police Department are committed to excellence in law enforcement and are dedicated to the people, traditions, culture and way of life in our community. In order to carry out duties, we will maintain professional, ethical, compassionate service to our community members. We will administer the Law in a fair and equitable manner, ensuring that victims of crime remain our focus. We shall provide a proactive approach to combat crime in our community by the use of community policing initiatives, creating a strong bond between community and law enforcement. We are committed to the idea of being part of the community that we serve."[26]

. . . .

26. Lac du Flambeau Tribal Police Department, "Mission Statement" (presented to Fox Valley Technical College, Appleton, WI, January 30, 2013).

Oneida Tribe of Indians of Wisconsin

About the Tribe

The Oneida Nation, situated on 65,000 acres in two counties located in Northeastern Wisconsin, has 233 miles of streams and more than 12,000 acres of wetlands.[27] The land is primarily used for agriculture. Although the tribe's population exceeds 27,700, there are 16,700 enrolled members, 4,200 of whom reside on the reservation. The tribe has "three levels of government: general tribal council, a business committee, and the tribal judicial system."[28]

Website: www.oneida-nsn.gov

Overview

The tribe hosted the TTEAMS training on September 13–14, 2011. Attendees from the Oneida Nation included community members and representatives from the tribe's law enforcement, behavioral health, children and family services, emergency management, the employee assistance program, and housing authority. Also, representatives from the Brown County Juvenile Court Services, the Wisconsin Indian Tribal Community Reintegration Program, and the Seymour Community School District were in attendance. The training provided opportunities for attendees to learn community policing practices, to get to know one another better, and to improve efficiency in providing resources to the community.

In 1994, the Oneida Housing Authority, after noticing gang graffiti at one of the housing sites, contacted the police department, and together they reached out to other service providers and community members to create the Oneida Gang Task Force to address gang problems. With no official charter, the task force solicited donations to host several events, such as the week-long Culture Camps, and took part in the National Night Out and "Take Back the Site." After several years, gang problems appeared to have subsided, although the task force used no definitive measurements other than a "look around" the community. Consequently, the volunteer task force somewhat disbanded.

In 2010, a criminal case involving a gang-related beating and stolen vehicle galvanized the almost nonexistent task force to renew its efforts in addressing this and other gang issues. The Oneida Police Department gave a presentation about community challenges to the Oneida Business Committee and other tribal leaders. In May 2010, the committee passed a formal resolution to establish the Oneida Gang Prevention Task Force, which included service providers whom the tribe's joint executive team and community members newly appointed to the group.

The TTEAMS training assisted attendees in developing a formal action plan to continue addressing gang issues. In December 2011, community members conducted an assessment of gang issues and asked youths, adults, social service workers, detention staff, and the police about gang activity. The study confirmed that gang problems were still prevalent, and so the Gang Prevention Task Force formally changed its name to the Oneida Community Action Team to reflect its philosophy of addressing long-term issues instead of a short-term "fix."

Strategy to Address Gangs

The community's goal is to reduce gang activity through prevention, education, and suppression through the following action steps and activities:

1. **Form the Community Action Team.**
    a. Identify key stakeholders and potential members who may be interested.
    b. Send invitation to potential members.
    c. Establish goals, and identify desired outcomes of the community action group.
    d. Identify roles and responsibilities of the community action group members.
    e. Schedule regular meetings, and set meeting agenda for each meeting.

**ONEIDA POLICE
CITIZENS ACADEMY**

*FOR THOSE INTERESTED IN LEARNING ABOUT
"THE CAREER OF A POLICE OFFICER" AND A
CHANCE TO GIVE BACK TO YOUR
COMMUNITY*

- 8 WEEK COMMITMENT
- MINIMUM AGE -18 YEARS OLD
- MUST PASS BACKGROUND CHECK
- COMPLETE & SUBMIT APPLICATION

~DEADLINE TO APPLY – MARCH 16th 2012~

FOR FURTHER DETAILS CONTACT OFFICER MATT KINKAN/OFFICE
920-969-6661 OR EMAIL / MKINKAN2 // ONEIDANATION.ORG

▲ *The Oneida Police Department created the Citizens' Police Academy marketing flyer that it distributes to the local tribal newspaper; area businesses such as Wal-Mart and gas stations; and other local departments such as education, social services, and recreation. Local community leaders also distribute the information to viable candidates.*

27. Velarde Tiller, *Tiller's Guide to Indian Country*, 1053.

28. "Oneida Tribal Government," Oneida Tribe of Indians of Wisconsin, 2013, www.oneida-nsn.gov.

2. **Develop a two-fold prevention and education strategy.**
   a. Identify service providers to help develop the strategy.
   b. Discuss potential root causes.
   c. Develop prevention and education efforts.

3. **Create and implement a Community Action Team coordinator position.**
   a. Define position and responsibilities, and create a job description.
   b. Post job announcement.
   c. Interview candidates.
   d. Hire and train employee.
   e. Conduct regular meetings with the coordinator to discuss progress/needs.
   f. Monitor the coordinator's efforts to provide education and intervention opportunities for the community.

4. **Create and implement a community resource officer position.**
   a. Define the position and responsibilities, and create a job description.
   b. Post the job announcement.
   c. Interview candidates.
   d. Hire and train officer.
   e. Conduct regular meetings with the community resource officer to discuss progress/needs.

5. **Develop variety of prevention programs directed toward youths.**
   a. Develop a planning team.
   b. Conduct youth focus group.
   c. Explore potential prevention programming ideas.
   d. Identify program leads/teams.
   e. Solicit necessary program materials (e.g., boxing gloves, basketballs, and uniforms) from community organizations, agencies, businesses.

Outcomes to date

1. **Form the Community Action Team.**

   The community formed a 24-member action group to help collaborate and coordinate efforts to address gang issues. The Oneida Police Department funds and supervises the Community Action Team coordinator. Team members include representatives from housing authority, grants department, human resources, land management department, the tribal council, gaming, social services, the police department, recreation, public works, the Oneida Nation School System, and Oneida Law Office. The group shares information about gang-related situations and collaborates on community-related events that enable the team to educate the community about the importance of prevention and intervention. The group meets monthly, and tribal departments learn to collaborate more and lean on each other for assistance. Typically, the departments face similar issues, so working together allows them to share resources and manpower, enabling them to better resolve the issues and enhance community programs.

   The current leadership and board members are progressively working to implement gang-prevention strategies and educational programs and are working on a tribal-wide gang graffiti removal policy. The group is also involved in numerous community-related events sponsored by the Oneida Police Department.

2. **Develop a two-fold prevention and education strategy.**

To address possible root causes for gang involvement, the group developed prevention strategies and educational programs. One major cause identified was that youths have little or no support system in their homes. The police department began an educational program that focuses on helping parents realize the influential role they have in their children's lives.

Prevention efforts led by the Oneida Police Department focused on providing ongoing information to youths about making good decisions and lifestyle choices. By mentoring youth and encouraging good choices, the police department hopes to stem the need for more stringent efforts at a later time. In addition, the police department participated in community-related events, educated youth about the risks of drugs and being involved in gang activity, and created positive relationships with the youths.

The school and Community Action Team offer additional programs. The school, with assistance from the police department and other tribal departments, provides healthier life-style programs such as athletics, educational clubs, after-school activities, college exploration, leadership and mentorship programs, and college and career exploration. The Community Action Team coordinator organizes educational opportunities for the youths. This involves taking a traditional approach where the coordinator and occasionally community experts teach the youths about their culture and heritage, helping them to embrace their culture and not gang-related practices.

3. **Create and implement a Community Action Team coordinator position.**

An integral component to success in the program, the coordinator is responsible for overseeing the meetings, setting the agenda, assigning tasks, and monitoring the action steps to ensure timely completion. Because so many departments serve on the team, the coordinator serves as a facilitator for open communication and provides resource assistance pertaining to issues identified by the team. The coordinator understands the variables in program operations and appreciates personalities, both of which assist in creating a more effective committee. In addition, the coordinator is familiar with the resources of all tribal departments as well as how to connect service providers to knock down previous "silos."

4. **Create and implement a community resource officer position.**

The police department created a position for a community resource officer whose sole responsibility is to coordinate the community's gang prevention and suppression efforts. The department's chief of police, Richard Van Boxtel, believes this position is essential because the officer can interact with nearby agencies, serve as a point of contact for other tribal and nontribal departments, use creative approaches, and be influential in his or her job duties. This officer can make the biggest, most positive impact by utilizing all components of community policing. This includes outreach to the community and building bridges with at-risk youths and the community.

The community resource officer has been instrumental in developing, engaging in, or soliciting participation in numerous community-based programs, such as the following:

- Cops and Bobbers (a fishing event for youths)
- Shop with a Cop during Christmas
- Reading with Officer Matt at the library
- Green Bay Police Multi-Jurisdictional Police Academy
- Neighborhood watch meetings
- Super Bowl of Safety at Lambeau Field (professional football stadium)
- Use of "Safe Assured ID" (a child identification system that stores fingerprints, photos, and video images) at area events
- National Night Out
- "Native Gangs and Drugs" training (to improve community awareness)

The community resource officer also is an active member of the Native American Drug and Gang Initiative (NADGI), which is a partnership among Wisconsin tribal law enforcement agencies and the Wisconsin Department of Justice, Division of Criminal Investigation with the goal of combatting drug and gang activity on the reservations.

5. **Create a variety of prevention programs directed toward youths.**

   The community crafted a variety of prevention programs geared toward all youths, not just at-risk youths:

   - **Cultural Camp:** The Community Action Team, in partnership with the Oneida Police Department; the Oneida Nation's Cultural Department, Housing Authority, and Recreation Department; and Oneida Longhouse[29] members facilitate a weeklong Oneida Culture Camp for middle and high school youth twice during the summer. At the camp, spiritual leaders speak about Oneida culture, heritage, and language to give youths a sense of identity and ways that Native peoples define themselves in today's world. The camp also focuses on building life skills and offers fun social events. Approximately 50 youths attend the camp every year.

   - **Champions Basketball:** Twenty-two youth members are involved in an ongoing basketball program to build upon and improve their lifestyle choices and decision-making skills, as well as their basic basketball skills. The program is held at the tribal recreation center and led by the community resource officer. Youth not only learn positive traits but also participate in community improvements, such as repainting the community's recreation center. Of the 22 members, four recently graduated high school and started their college education. Two members are currently playing Division 2 college basketball, and one member is playing Division 2 collegiate lacrosse. One female member who is still in high school is the Junior Miss Oneida—a position that also makes her a spokeswoman for the Oneida Tribe and involves her in various events. The police department is very proud of these members who are becoming future leaders.

- - - - - - - - - - - - - - - -

29. According to Ron Hill Sr. of the Oneida Cultural Heritage Department, the Oneida Longhouse, or "Longhouse," is both an actual structure (historically a multifamily dwelling) and the name of the Oneida traditional culture and spiritual way of life. Today, the Longhouse holds traditional ceremonies including social dances and gatherings.

- **Bike Rodeo:** This event brought youths together in a positive environment to promote respect for laws and for each other. The bike rodeo, for children and their family members, is held three times a year and sponsored by the Oneida Housing Authority and the Oneida Police Department, provides a bicycle mechanical checkup, bike riding skills, and an explanation of the community's rights and responsibilities when riding a bicycle in traffic. As such, the department promotes wearing bicycle helmets and safe bike riding practices.

- **Blanket Making:** During Christmas time, police, fire, and EMS employees, along with community members and youths, spend a morning making blankets for community members in need. Some blankets are given to youths who in turn must give the blankets to a community member who previously helped them or made a difference in their lives.

- **Take 25:** The National Center for Missing and Exploited Children (NCMEC) created this child safety campaign in honor of National Missing Children's Day, which is annually observed on May 25th. The campaign raises awareness about issues surrounding missing and exploited children and helps educate communities about the risks children face. Take 25 (www.take25.org) provides communities with free safety resources, including safety tips, conversation starters, and engaging activities; and encourages parents, guardians, educators, and others to take 25 minutes to talk with children about safety. The Oneida tribal community participates in this nationwide campaign each year.

These programs provide youths with alternatives to being involved in gangs and criminal activity. They also enable law enforcement officers to serve as mentors and be positive role models for the youths. As a result of the programs, youths have a more positive attitude, and some at-risk youth have become productive members and moved away from a criminal lifestyle.

The police department also saw a 70 percent reduction in gang graffiti in 2012 compared to 2010 and 2011. Comparing 2006 (a peak year) to 2011, the number of juvenile arrests dropped by more than half. Likewise, adult arrests dropped in the same period by 15 percent.

Lessons Learned

To be effective, both council leadership and community leaders must have "buy-in." Using a methodical approach to involve everyone across the broad community spectrum and to "knock down silos" is important to improving the community.

When implementing a community resource officer position, the officer must be well-versed and trained in community oriented policing and problem solving. Necessary training also includes drug investigations, gang investigations, domestic crimes, search warrants, development, and education.

Additional Community Policing Activities

The police department hosts a citizens' police academy for community members. The academy meets once a year for eight consecutive, weekly sessions. The minimum age requirement is 18, and applicants must pass a background check. Attendees learn about police work, traffic enforcement, firearms, defensive tactics, and community policing.

Contact Information
_____

Oneida Police Department
2783 Freedom Road
Oneida, WI 54155
Ph: 920-869-2239 (office)
Fax: 920-869-1864
Website: www.oneidanation.org/policedepartment

Lead Contacts
_____

Rich Van Boxtel, Chief of Police | rvanboxtel@oneidanation.org

Matt Ninham, Community Resource Officer | mninham2@oneidanation.org

Lead Agency Demographics
_____

The Oneida Police Department, initially called the Oneida Public Safety Department, was established in 1985 with a chief of police, 13 officers, and one secretary/dispatcher.[30] All officers were tribal members, and "the intention was to provide police, fire, and rescue services to the reservation."[31]

Currently, the police department has 31 employees with 22 sworn officers. It has a full-time dispatch center, and detention services are contracted out to surrounding counties. The department also has a DARE officer in the elementary school, a community resource officer, a school liaison/DARE officer in the high school, and two canine units.

Mission Statement

"The Oneida Police Department serves the community, within the Oneida reservation, by helping build a stronger, safer community through police protection and service while instilling a sense of unity and treating all with respect, dignity, and compassion."[32]

. . . .

30. "About Us," Oneida Tribe of Indians of Wisconsin, 2013, www.oneidanation.org/policedepartment/aboutus.aspx.

31. Ibid.

32. Ibid.

Puyallup Tribe

About the Tribe

The Puyallup Indians, who have "lived along the shores of Puget Sound, Washington, for many years, were known as the S'Puyalupubsh, which means generous and welcoming behavior to all people (friends and strangers) who enter their lands."[33] The reservation is located south of Seattle within Pierce County. In recent years, the tribe's population has grown and is now approximately 4,000–4,500 people, with two-thirds of its members living on the reservation in nearby Tacoma.[34] The tribe is the third largest employer in the county in the areas of fishing, transportation, finance, real estate, healthcare, education, social services, recreation, and entertainment.

Website: www.puyallup-tribe.com

Overview

The Puyallup tribal community hosted the TTEAMS training on April 13–14, 2011. Attendees from the Puyallup Tribe included its law enforcement, community family services, counseling services, courts, housing, behavioral health, employment rights, and planning and land services. In addition, representatives from the City of Tacoma Human Rights and Human Services, Tacoma community groups, South Puget Intertribal Planning Agency, Tacoma-Pierce County Health Department, and Washington State Department of Corrections were also in attendance.

The tribe chose to use the training information to strengthen community partnerships to better address two key challenges in the community: alcohol and substance abuse and gangs, specifically in the First Creek housing area that houses mainly nonmembers of the tribe. The ultimate goal is to help community members become healthier in both mind and body.

Strategy to Address Alcohol and Substance Abuse and Gang Issues

The tribal community felt that through education and a sharing of ideas, they could come to a better understanding of the issues surrounding alcohol and substance abuse as well as gang activity. As a result, the community identified the following strategy to focus on addressing alcohol and substance abuse as well as promoting awareness, prevention, and direct intervention efforts to address gang issues:

1. **Enhance communication and relationships with key stakeholders.**
    a. Plan an open community forum for tribal members to discuss key community concerns and safety issues.
        i. Identify dates and a location to hold the forum.
        ii. Select a moderator for the forum.
        iii. Identify someone to record the minutes/discussion.
        iv. Invite community members and key stakeholders to participate.
    b. Develop an advisory board to address identified community issues.
        i. Invite representatives from key stakeholders / tribal agencies to join the advisory board.
        ii. Schedule the first meeting.
            — Select or nominate an advisory board chair/leader.
            — Develop vision and mission statements.
            — Discuss short- and long-term goals of the advisory board.

33. "Welcome," Puyallup Tribe of Indians, 2013, www.puyallup-tribe.com.
34. Ibid.

— Discuss current resources and services available through various service provider agencies, and identify areas for collaboration. After the meeting, collect further information, and develop a resource guide (to be located at each provider agency) with agency information, available services, and contact information.

— Establish a regular meeting schedule.

2. **Form a gang task force.**

   a. Communicate information about developing a task force to key stakeholders in the community.

   b. Invite selected members to the initial meeting.

   c. After identifying and confirming the Gang Task Force members, establish regular core meetings.

      i. Assess the level of current gang activity.

      ii. Identify potential underlying causes or root issues.

      iii. Identify existing prevention and intervention efforts that can be promoted or enhanced.

      iv. Propose new efforts.

      v. Determine financial needs and resources.

      vi. Recruit volunteers to work on prevention or intervention efforts if necessary.

3. **Transition the established task force into the Tribal Community Alliance.**

   a. Reach out to Gang Task Force members to gauge their interest in the new Community Alliance program.

   b. Invite new members.

   c. Identify alliance leader(s).

   d. Define the roles of members.

   e. Review the mission and vision statements, and revise as necessary.

   f. Define or redefine the goals and objectives of the alliance.

   g. Establish regular meetings to identify alcohol-, drug-, and gang-free activities/events that can be organized and Identify members to help plan and organize each event.

4. **Implement a knock-and-talk program.**

   a. Identify at-risk youths and parents in the community through discussions with school staff and parents or guardians.

   b. Obtain parental consent to visit the home to meet with their children.

   c. Meet with other agencies to identify prevention, intervention, and available educational resources, and bring this information to home visits.

   d. Share information and pamphlets on drug-free activities and programs with youths during home visits.

5. **Reinstate the police explorer program.**

   a. Review the curriculum, and make any necessary revisions or updates.

   b. Identify officers and instructors who will participate and serve as mentors.

   c. Schedule dates and location(s).

   d. Distribute marketing information to middle and high schools, local colleges and universities, parents, etc.

   e. Share registration information and eligibility requirements.

    f.   Purchase any necessary equipment, supplies, or uniforms.

    g. Consider how to revise the program to avoid explorers from being viewed as police informants because they participated in the program.

Outcomes to Date

1. **Enhance communication and relationships with key stakeholders.**

   After the TTEAMS training, the community experienced renewed communication among stakeholders and was better educated and informed about community policing issues. It also had a more profound understanding of the issues confronting their community. More information sharing, less duplication of efforts between groups, and a greater appreciation of others' viewpoints provided a renewed and more-coordinated focus on gang and substance abuse issues.

   The Puyallup Tribal Police Department renewed its commitment to community policing. As a result, it upgraded its training, and its relationships with other tribal entities have allowed more diverse viewpoints and understanding when addressing common issues.

   Although the community is somewhat isolated in the region, significant services and resources are available through the Community/Family Services Program to help community members address substance abuse. Officers are now better able to refer individuals in need to the appropriate services because the police department enhanced its relationship with other tribal agencies, resulting in more frequent use of resources such as the Community/Family Services Program.

2. **Form a gang task force.**

   The Puyallup Tribe formed a gang task force comprising representatives from various tribal services divisions such as law enforcement, family services, the tribal council, and health services in addition to community members. The task force meets once or twice a year to review needs and issues and to discuss new ideas. The Puyallup Tribal Police Department's Gang Unit is also a component of the regional task force comprising multiple law enforcement agencies in Pierce County. The regional task force provides enforcement and suppression efforts and shares information, intelligence, and resources to address gang activity in the region. Each agency assigns officers to the regional task force as an auxiliary duty.

   In 2012, the Pierce County Multi-Agency Regional Gang Task Force, which includes the Puyallup Tribal Police Department, received a Thrasher Award from the National Gang Crime Research Center for "superior service in gang prevention."

   The tribe's gang task force later transitioned into the Tribal Community Alliance, which is discussed in the following outcome to date.

3. **Transition the established task force into the Tribal Community Alliance.**

   The community established the Tribal Community Alliance whose mission is to provide healthy, sober, and gang-free events and education for the entire local community. Representatives in the alliance include tribal elders, staff from the tribe's family services program and child protective services, government agencies, and law enforcement with significant tribal council support. The core group meets on a monthly basis, and the full team meets twice a year to review and adjust the community's efforts. The Tribal Community Alliance has organized the annual Christmas parade and a National Night Out event.

The annual Christmas parade includes a tree lighting at the health clinic followed by hot chocolate and snacks at the Kwawachee Spirit House. After a two-year hiatus, the Christmas Parade resumed in 2011 and most recently took place on December 14, 2012. Spectators ranged in age from newborns to elders, and parade participants distributed candy, ornaments, and other holiday trinkets.

The Tribal Community Alliance, along with the Set Aside Housing Program, organized a National Night Out on August 2, 2011 to bring community members and neighbors together in a positive way while also taking a stance against local crime. The event included educational outreach booths sponsored by various community groups, dinner, and fun activities for children. Approximately 250 people, including dozens of families, attended the event and received a T-shirt that read, "Coming Together is a Beginning; Keeping Together is Progress; Working Together is a Success (Henry Ford)." This quote reiterates the alliance's mission to unify the community.

4. **Implement a knock-and-talk program.**

   The police department encouraged a community outreach effort called "knock and talk" (i.e., police making home visits) to start preventative interventions for youths going astray. These educational visits are for those at-risk youths who were identified through current police contacts and referrals from school authorities and parents.

5. **Reinstate the police explorer program.**

   The Puyallup Tribal Police Department's police explorer program was dormant for a while, but after the TTEAMS training, the department thought the program to be an instrumental part of community oriented policing. Approximately 15–20 youths actively participated in the program, and, as a result, the department noted lower gang involvement.

   The department is currently revising the program because gang members thought several explorers were police informants. As such, the department is currently evaluating ways to keep program participants from being harassed.

Additional Community Policing Activities

The tribe created both a community garden for provisions and a medicine garden to bring back traditional healing methods and tools.

The police department's revived reserve officer program has grown from five positions and a chaplain to 10 positions. Reserve officers serve as a second officer in a car, doubling the manpower available for patrol and special activities.

The Puyallup Tribe of Indians is a supporter of the Northwest Gang Investigators Association. Gang officers, school staff, and social services staff receive training through this program.

The Puyallup Tribe of Indians also hosted the National Gang Center training titled "Gangs in Indian County" in March 2012.

Lessons Learned

The police reported that as they embraced the community policing initiative, their efforts snowballed and gained momentum throughout the community.

Community policing training helped the police department increase networking opportunities, enabling the police to utilize tribal resources better, and more tribal executives and leaders have become involved.

Contact Information

Puyallup Tribal Police Department
1638 E 29th Street
Tacoma, WA 98404
Ph: 253-680-5656 (office)
Fax: 253-680-5659
Website: www.puyallup-tribe.com/law-enforcement/puyallup_tribal_police_department

Lead Contact

William Loescher, Patrol Lieutenant and Gang Unit Supervisor |
william.loescher@puyalluptribe.com

Lead Agency Demographics

The police department formed in 1974 and was cross-commissioned with the state in 1990. There are 30 sworn positions, 10 corrections officers, and four civilian positions. Two officers are school resource officers, and one of them is also a Gang Resistance Education and Training (GREAT) instructor. Seven officers function as an ancillary gang unit.

Mission Statement

"It is the mission of the Puyallup Tribal Police Department to safeguard life and property, to enforce Tribal law in a fair and impartial manner, to preserve peace and order within the boundaries of the Puyallup Reservation, and to aggressively pursue this mission in conformance with the culture and values of the Puyallup Tribe of Indians."[35]

. . . .
35. "Puyallup Tribal Police Department Mission Statement," Puyallup Tribe of Indians, 2013, www.puyallup-tribe.com/law-enforcement/puyallup_tribal_police_department/.

Chitimacha Tribe of Louisiana
About the Tribe

The Chitimacha reservation is located in south central Louisiana in St. Mary Parish, near the town of Charenton and southeast of Lafayette.[36] The Chitimacha Tribe is the only tribe in Louisiana to still occupy a portion of their aboriginal homeland.[37] The tribe comprises four bands: the Chitimacha, Yagenechito (eastern Chitimacha), Chawasha, and Washa.[38] Today, tribal membership is approximately 950, and approximately 350 members reside on the Chitimacha reservation.[39] The crown jewel of the Chitimacha cultural tradition is river cane basketry, both single and double woven. According to tribal legend, a deity taught basketry to the Chitimacha, and tribal families have been practicing this art for thousands of years. The more than 50 different design elements can be combined to create hundreds of different basket designs.

The Chitimacha constitution and bylaws have been in place since September 1970.[40] The council that governs the tribe consists of a chairman, vice-chairman, secretary, and two other members, all elected to two-year terms. The Chitimacha's enterprises in agricultural, fishing, and gaming industries sustain the tribe's economy. Additional enterprises include Cypress Bayou Casino Hotel, Raintree Market, Raintree Village (master plan development property), Keta Group, LLC (a holding company), Tiya Support Services (a governmental contracting company), Colorado Professional Resources, LLC (a technical support company that supports U.S. Department of Defense agencies), and Tiya Construction Services, LLC.

The tribal council adopted the following mission statement to define the responsibilities of the tribe's people:

> We, the people of the Sovereign Nation of the Chitimacha, in order to proclaim and perpetuate our vision, hereby embrace these beliefs:

> - We must preserve and protect our natural resources, our people, and all Native Americans;

> - We must promote a harmonious existence among ourselves, and within our community;

> - We must maintain the highest level of integrity, honor, and authenticity in all of our endeavors; and

> - We must always exist as a Nation by preserving our cultural heritage.[41]

Website: www.chitimacha.gov

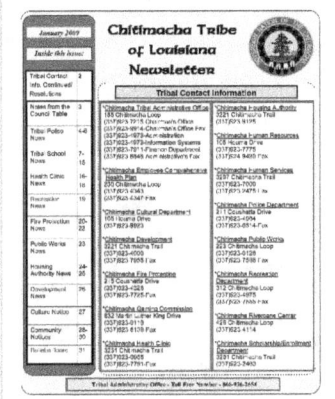

▲ A section of the Chitimacha quarterly tribal newsletter is dedicated to updates and news from the tribal police department. News may include citations and arrests, updates on codes of justice, officer trainings and certifications received, and upcoming activities sponsored by the police department such as its ATV safety class.

. . . .

36. Velarde Tiller, *Tiller's Guide to Indian Country*, 559.

37. "History," Chitimacha Tribe of Louisiana, 2013, www.chitimacha.gov/tribal_about_history.htm.

38. Velarde Tiller, *Tiller's Guide to Indian Country*, 559.

39. "History," Chitimacha Tribe of Louisiana, 2013, www.chitimacha.gov/tribal_about_history.htm.

40. "Chitimacha Tribe of Louisiana—Tribal Government," Chitimacha Tribe of Louisiana, 2013, www.chitimacha.gov/tribal_government.htm.

41. "The Chitimacha Tribal Council," Chitimacha Tribe of Louisiana, 2005, www.chitimacha.gov/tribal_council.htm.

Overview

The Chitimacha Tribe hosted the TTEAMS training on December 16–17, 2009. Attendees from the Chitimacha Tribe included representatives from law enforcement, fire protection, courts, and human services. During the training, attendees explored strategies and options to further strengthen community safety programs. The three main themes identified during the training were as follows:

1. The police department noted a decline in participation at community meetings.
2. The tribe identified substance abuse issues.
3. The community recognized substance abuse issues related to alcohol, marijuana, cocaine, and prescription drugs.

Following the training, the Chitimacha Tribal Police Department began to explore strategies to develop stronger relationships with the community and increase participation at community meetings and police department-sponsored events, including those intended to address substance abuse.

Strategy to Address Community Involvement

As a result of the training, attendees identified strategies for how law enforcement could become more familiar with the community and how it could address the community's concerns more effectively.

The tribal police department served as the lead agency for implementing the strategies, scheduling and planning activities and ensuring community members were actively involved, and took the following steps:

1. **Attend a grandparent and parent summit as part of the parish-wide Red Ribbon Week activities.**
   a. Identify summit dates and a location.
   b. Identify summit agenda topics and presenters.
   c. Identify ways to market the summit to the community.
   d. Distribute information about the summit to the community.

2. **Assist with a Halloween carnival sponsored by the tribal school.**
   a. Identify local agencies and businesses that could support the carnival and provide donations.
   b. Plan carnival events.
      i. Create activities to involve youths.
      ii. Identify themes associated with the activities.
      iii. Advertise the events.

3. **Assist with organizing Red Ribbon Week.**
   a. Invite local departments and government agencies to participate in a motorcade through the parish.
   b. Plan a route for the motorcade.
   c. Advertise the event to the community.

4. **Organize a canoe/kayak bayou run.**
   a. Select dates to hold the canoe/kayak river run.
   b. Plan a route.
   c. Invite participants.
   d. Advertise the event.

5. **Hold all-terrain vehicle (ATV) safety classes for youths.**
   a. Identify class instructors.
   b. Develop class curriculum.
   c. Set class rules.
   d. Identify dates and location(s) to hold the classes.
   e. Distribute class information to parents and the community.

6. **Organize a National Night Out event.**
   a. Determine the target audience.
   b. Schedule date(s) for National Night Out.
   c. Identify local businesses and agencies that could provide donations and support.
   d. Identify event activities and ways to involve youths.
   e. Invite community members and the target audience.

7. **Conduct a tour of Angola Prison (i.e., Louisiana State Penitentiary).**
   a. Establish the goals of the tour.
   b. Identify the audience and targeted age group.
   c. Propose a plan to the prison and the school, and achieve their buy-in.
   d. Identify prisoners to speak about life choices during the tour.
   e. Schedule tour dates.

Outcomes to Date

The Chitimacha Tribe has been successful in implementing community policing activities, and the following summarizes its progress on key activities and strategies:

1. **Attend a grandparent and parent summit as part of the parish-wide Red Ribbon Week activities.**

   The community recognized that youths were increasingly abusing bath salts to get high. In response, the Chitimacha Tribal Police Department assists other agencies with coordinating a grandparent and parent summit to educate the community about the dangers of abusing bath salts. The police department's juvenile officer, who handles all juvenile incidences and complaints for the department, teaches the Drug Abuse Resistance Education (DARE) program at the tribal school and speaks to students about the rising use of drugs, such as bath salts, and their dangers.

2. **Assist with a Halloween carnival sponsored by the tribal school.**

   The tribal school sponsors an annual carnival around Halloween that features rides, carnival games, educational booths, and a petting zoo. The police department provides security for the event, and officers interact with the community. Last year, approximately 300 community members attended. The local trading post sponsored a shopping bag coloring contest for local children with the theme "Don't waste your treasures on unfit pleasures." Afterward, many residents sought out these specifically themed, hand-colored bags that the trading post used to bag customers' purchases.

3. **Assist with organizing Red Ribbon Week.**

In October, the police department works with surrounding communities to hold a four-hour motorcade through the entire parish to support Red Ribbon Week, one of the largest drug prevention campaigns in the country (www.imdrugfree. com). More than 150 people and 70 emergency vehicles from local government agencies participate in this annual event. Each year, the motorcade travels a different route; one year, the route runs east to west, and the next year, it runs west to east. This provides community members from the surrounding communities with an opportunity to participate in and/or observe the motorcade. The police department's juvenile officer coordinates an activity at the tribal school where students draw on grocery bags obtained from the local trading post to show their support of Red Ribbon Week. The bags are then returned to the trading post for bagging purchased items. The drug-free theme for this annual activity changes each year. One example was "Don't waste your treasures on unfit pleasures."

4. **Organize a canoe/kayak bayou run.**

For the past three years, the tribe participated in a three-day canoe/kayak bayou run coordinated by Tour du Teche (www.tourduteche.com). A one-day mini-race for children under 16 years of age also takes place in conjunction with this event. The Bayou Teche runs through tribal land, and access to the bayou is closed to normal boating traffic during the event. Officers make a point to mingle with and greet the participants when they stop at the local tribal boat landing, and their presence also provides additional security for the participants.

5. **Hold all-terrain vehicle (ATV) safety classes for youths.**

ATV safety is a big concern for the community, as many youths ride on vacant tribal lands. The Chitimacha Tribal Police Department now offers a four-hour ATV safety class twice a year on Saturdays that provides basic safety instruction for youths ages 16 and under. While a parent or legal guardian must accompany children below the age of 12, children between the ages 12 and 16 may attend on their own. When officers see youths riding ATVs unsafely, they encourage those youths to attend the next safety class, and a total of nine youths and their parents attended the last class. If youths successfully complete the class, they receive an ATV safety card that allows them to operate their ATV on the roadway in a slow and safe manner.

6. **Organize a National Night Out event.**

The police department held a community-wide National Night Out event for the past four years. Due to the heat in August, the event is usually held inside the school gym. Various tribal groups attend, including victim rights advocates, local domestic violence shelter staff members, and human services groups. The success of the event is due largely to local donations.

The police department sets up inflatable jumping amusements (or bounce house) and a petting zoo to encourage youth attendance. This event also includes food, music, games, and a table set up with various educational materials on safety issues such as identity theft and the dangers of using drugs and alcohol. Many residents from the reservation and surrounding community attend the event, and the turnout continues to increase every year.

7. **Conduct a tour of Angola Prison (i.e., Louisiana State Penitentiary).**

The tour at the state penitentiary has been an annual event for graduating eighth graders for the past three years. During the field trip, juveniles hear from inmates about the lifestyle choices that got them in trouble, the consequences of their crimes, and the lessons they learned from their mistakes. The inmates encourage the youths to make good decisions that will allow them to lead a crime-free life. This field trip supplements the regular DARE program offered to the 90 students in the tribal school, including students in pre-kindergarten through eighth grade.

In summary, the Chitimacha Tribal Police Department has reported stronger community involvement, and the officers have become more aware of community members' concerns. The residents eagerly anticipate the police department-sponsored events, and participation in the events has greatly increased.

Lessons Learned

Captain Hebert of the Chitimacha Tribal Police Department suggested that when holding annual events, such as National Night Out, something new should be added each year to "change things up and make it livelier." He also recommended the use of door prizes and food to encourage more participation and create interest. It is important to be prepared and not be discouraged when some individuals do not show up as promised. Despite reservations or RSVPs, "things will happen," and some residents won't be able to attend.

Additional Community Policing Activities

In addition to the activities and strategies discussed, the chief of police encourages his officers to meet with and learn more about the residents. Patrol officers are assigned certain streets in the residential area of the reservation with the expectation that they meet the citizens and hear their concerns. Residents can fill out a survey that asks various questions about how the police are handling their complaints and what they would like the police department to do more of to assist them.

The police actively contribute to the *Chitimacha Tribe of Louisiana Newsletter*. They write articles about important community concerns, list police actions from the past month, provide more insight into the department, and include information about scheduled activities. For example, information about the ATV safety class is published in the newsletter.

Contact Information

Chitimacha Tribal Police Department
PO Box 700
Charenton, LA 70523
Ph: 337-923-4964 (office)
Fax: 337-923-0514

Lead Contacts

Blaise Smith, Chief of Police | blaise@chitimacha.gov

Ellen Hebert, Captain | ellen@chitimacha.gov

Lead Agency Demographics

The Chitimacha Tribal Police Department comprises 14 full-time employees and six additional reserve officers. The department has five dispatchers; seven officers, which includes a juvenile officer; a captain; and the chief of police.

Mission Statement

The Chitimacha Tribal Police Department's mission is "to safeguard lives and property of all residents of the Chitimacha Indian Reservation while preserving their constitutional rights. Various responsibilities correspond to this mission. All officers will make these departmental responsibilities their own and will not allow personal feelings, animosities, prejudices, or personal relationships to influence their decisions. All officers will diligently and courteously carry out their duties and responsibilities and take pride in the services they provide." [42]

. . . .
42. Chitimacha Tribal Police Department, "Mission Statement" (presented to Fox Valley Technical College, Appleton, WI, October 4, 2012).

Fond du Lac Band of Lake Superior Chippewa

About the Tribe

The Fond du Lac Reservation, one of six Chippewa Indian reservations in the state of Minnesota, is organized as the Minnesota Chippewa Tribe.[43] The reservation, which covers 156 square miles in Carlton and St. Louis counties, is adjacent to the city of Cloquet on the east and 15 miles west of Duluth. The tribe has 4,500 members, and its tribal government comprises the Reservation Business Committee with five elected officials, three of whom represent the reservation's three districts. The tribe operates more than 40 separate programs, such as education, social and health services, economic development, and conservation, as well as its own tribal court system.

Overview

The Fond du Lac reservation hosted the TTEAMS training on October 4–5, 2010. Attendees from the Fond du Lac Band of Lake Superior Chippewa included representatives from its law enforcement, human services, behavioral health, housing, compliance, and the community center. Representatives from the Carlton County Sheriff's Office and Carlton County Probation Office also attended. Although the reservation has an extensive selection of programs, community involvement in these programs has been low. After the TTEAMS training, the attendee's efforts focused on increasing community members' awareness of tribal issues and participation in programs.

Strategy to Address Community Involvement

The tribe opted to expand its efforts in three areas to enhance community involvement, and the Fond du Lac Police Department implemented the strategies by taking the following key steps and actions:

1. **Increase awareness about gangs by holding community meetings.**
   a. Identify the target audience.
   b. Identify a meeting location and dates.
   c. Prepare the meeting agenda and topics.

2. **Begin early stages of implementing a Neighborhood Watch Program.**
   a. Reach out to community members to gauge interest.
   b. Select meeting times and places to meet.
   c. Allow opportunity for citizens to discuss community concerns.
   d. Identify the comfort level of the community in reporting crime.
   e. Communicate safety and neighborhood watch information to the community when it is ready to be formally published.

3. **Enhance collaboration with the local sheriff's department.**
   a. Invite key stakeholders to the initial meeting.
   b. Identify the needs of the tribal police and sheriff's departments.
   c. Identify the benefits of collaboration for both agencies and communities.
   d. Identify representatives from both agencies who will be assigned to this process.
   e. Establish firm and regular meeting dates.
   f. Identify common problem(s) for the team to work on.
   g. Identify resources within both agencies and communities that can be used to address the problem(s) identified.

. . . .
43. "Fond du Lac Band of Lake Superior Chippewa," 2013, www.fdlrez.com.

Outcomes to Date

1. **Increase awareness about gangs by holding community meetings.**

   The Fond du Lac Police Department organized three gang awareness community meetings to explore gang-related issues and to raise awareness of the negative impacts of gangs infiltrating the community. These meetings were open to all community members to teach youths and elders about signs of gang involvement. Each meeting had approximately 100 attendees with standing room only; accordingly, the tribe is planning to find a larger facility for future meetings. The tribe's school resource officer assists in inviting speakers, organizing the presentations, and oversees the meetings.

   The police department sent an e-mail to all Fond du Lac tribal employees and other tribal departments, asking everyone to print and post a copy of the flyer to advertise the community meetings. At the end of each meeting, the police department distributed a survey to assess what the attendees understood, what information they absorbed related to gangs, what additional information they might need, and what type of additional educational opportunities they might be interested in. The survey responses indicated the community's desire to continue these types of meetings and related programs.

   Gang-related issues have decreased noticeably in the community since the implementation of the gang-awareness meetings.

2. **Begin the early stages of implementing a Neighborhood Watch Program.**

   The community is establishing a pilot Neighborhood Watch Program that involves approximately 15–25 homes in the community. Although the program is not yet fully developed, citizens are beginning to call and report what is happening in their community. One challenge in the implementation process—the relative isolation of some households—could limit the application of the program; however, the tribe plans to address this issue.

3. **Enhance collaboration with the local sheriff's department.**

   The Fond du Lac Police Department held meetings with the Carlton County Sheriff's Department; as a result, networking increased between the two agencies. They have also shared some resources, such as a list of individuals on probation or in chemical health treatment; names of pharmacists from whom the departments obtain information or notify about prescription drug issues; and the names of supportive housing advocates who are sharing information regarding gang and drug activity. The two departments signed a formal agreement to allow the deputy sheriffs to come onto the reservation to conduct investigations and respond to calls if needed. In situations where the sheriff's department is short-staffed, it can call the tribal police department to ask for assistance.

   Enhanced collaboration across jurisdictions has helped to address gang issues adequately within both Native and non-Native communities. The ability of tribal and nontribal law enforcement agencies to coordinate and collaborate on their enforcement actions and resources inhibits the movement of negative or criminal activity from one jurisdiction to another.

Lessons Learned

Information about gang recognition and identification in the beginning, specific to both the reservation and the community, would be extremely beneficial for all community members.

A police department must get to know its community members and what makes them comfortable and then work from there.

Additional Community Policing Activities

Overall, the police department ensures the presence of an officer at community events, and it promotes additional community policing activities.

Contact Information

Fond du Lac Police Department
930 Trettle Lane
Cloquet, MN 55720
Ph: 218-878-8040

Lead Contact

Vanessa Northrup, School Resource Officer | VanessaNorthrup@fdlrez.com

Lead Agency Demographics

The Fond du Lac Police Department operates 24 hours a day, seven days a week in the community and currently staffs police officers, a K-9 officer, clerical staff, and an animal control officer. It has assigned one officer as a school resource officer to work with the Fond du Lac Ojibwe Schools and students and has assigned another officer to investigations to work collaboratively with other area law enforcement officers and investigators. The police department also collaborates with the St. Louis County and Carlton County 911 Emergency Centers.[44]

Mission Statement

"We, the men and women of the Fond du Lac Law Enforcement believe that our fundamental duty is to serve and protect the citizens, resources, and cultural values of Fond du Lac Reservation with fairness, compassion, and respect. We demand excellence in the quality of our law enforcement, stressing professionalism, integrity, and timeliness, so that those we serve may feel secure. We provide equal enforcement and protection of the law without prejudice or favor. We promote the setting of goals in partnership with the community, and prioritize and address problems based on the concerns of the community. Committed to continuous improvement in law enforcement, we promote and utilize the most modern techniques available."[45]

---

44. "FDL Law Enforcement," Fond du Lac Band of Lake Superior Chippewa, 2013, www.fdlrez.com/police/main.htm.
45. Ibid.

Menominee Indian Tribe of Wisconsin

About the Tribe

The Menominee Tribe reservation, located in the Village of Keshena, approximately 45 miles northwest of Green Bay, Wisconsin, covers an estimated 350 square miles that span five main communities: Keshena, Neopit, Middle Village, Zoar, and South Branch.[46] The Menominee Tribal Legislature, which comprises nine members, including a chairperson and vice chairperson, governs the tribe.[47] The Menominee Tribe has more than 8,700 enrolled members of whom less than half live on the reservation due to lack of available housing and employment opportunities.

Website: www.menominee-nsn.gov

Overview

On November 29–30, 2011, the Menominee Tribal Police Department attended the TTEAMS training hosted by the Stockbridge Munsee Indian Community in Bowler, Wisconsin. Attendees learned about community oriented policing strategies and methods of developing partnerships to implement those strategies to address community challenges. Attendees from the Menominee Tribal Police Department identified the lack of community involvement as a main public safety concern. All too often, people have the mindset that crime is someone else's problem unless it happens to them or someone they know.

Strategy to Enhance Community Relationships and Involvement

The Menominee police team identified and created a strategy to improve outreach efforts by increasing the officers' visibility in the community through increased contact during patrol and Neighborhood Watch Programs. The additional outreach is intended to build trust and relationships with community members and to increase their interest in crime prevention and community policing efforts.

To accomplish their outreach efforts, the police team identified a need to implement Neighborhood Watch Programs. The Menominee Tribal Police Department served as the lead agency to ensure initiation and implementation of the strategy. As such, the department took the following steps:

1. **Implement Neighborhood Watch Programs.**

   a. Share information with other community service providers.

   b. Communicate regularly with the community through increased patrol efforts.

   c. Share information about watch programs in discussions and through written information.

   d. Assist interested communities in developing Neighborhood Watch Programs.

      i. Assist the community in selecting a watch program coordinator.

      ii. Attend the regularly scheduled meetings, which the watch program coordinator determines to be either monthly or quarterly, to provide updates and to ensure concerns are addressed.

   e. Help communities maintain their watch programs, and provide assistance whenever they seek help.

Outcomes to Date

1. **Implement Neighborhood Watch Programs.**

   The Menominee Tribal Police Department's goal is to establish Neighborhood Watch Programs in approximately 8–10 communities located on the reservation. In a one-year period, a total of two communities implemented successful programs. The communities held regular meetings, and when needed, they involved the police department or other service providers.

. . . .

46. "About Us," Menominee Indian Tribe of Wisconsin, 2013, www.menominee-nsn.gov/MITW/aboutUs.aspx.

47. Ibid.

Since the implementation of the programs, community members are more involved and willing to share their concerns with police officers. The police department credits the communities for the success of the programs and reported a 15–20 percent decrease in calls for service in those communities in a one-year period. The drop in calls for service can be attributed to the ability of the communities to address basic crime prevention needs.

The police department will continue to attend meetings and work with the communities that already have established watch programs. Furthermore, the department will continue its efforts to involve additional communities in the watch program.

Lessons Learned

According to Warren Warrington, master sergeant with the Menominee Tribal Police Department, establishing open communication between law enforcement and the community can be challenging. Having community members involved in the TTEAMS training and in planning the Neighborhood Watch Programs would have helped develop more open communication. However, since the establishment of the Neighborhood Watch Programs, community members are more willing to share information related to crime and suspicious activities.

Contact Information

Menominee Tribal Police Department
W3293 Wolf River Road
Keshena, WI 54135
Ph: 715-799-3321 (office)
Fax: 715-799-1310

Lead Contact

Warren Warrington, Master Sergeant | wwarrington@mitw.org

Lead Agency Demographics

The Menominee Tribal Police Department employs 46 people, including 25 sworn officers. The Law Enforcement Center also houses a detention facility that employs 16 staff, including administration, shift supervisors, correctional officers, and kitchen staff.[48]

Mission Statement

"The men and women of the Menominee Tribal Police Department are dedicated to enhancing the relationship between law enforcement and community members in order to build trust, reduce crime, build a proactive patrol, and create a safe community for current and future generations."[49]

. . . .

48. "Detention Facility—Mission Statement," Menominee Tribal Police Law Enforcement Center, 2013, http://metp.menominee-nsn.gov/Jail.aspx.

49. "Mission Statement," Menominee Tribal Police Law Enforcement Center, 2013, http://metp.menominee-nsn.gov.

Mississippi Band of Choctaw Indians

About the Tribe

The Choctaw Indian Reservation in east central Mississippi has approximately 10,000 members and covers 35,000 acres of trust land in 10 counties.[50] Each of the eight Choctaw Indian communities—Bogue Chitto, Bogue Homa, Conehatta, Crystal Ridge, Pearl River, Red Water, Standing Pine, and Tucker —is located between 15–90 miles from the largest community, Pearl River.[51] Fifty-three percent of the membership speaks the First Language.

Website: www.choctaw.org

Overview

The tribe hosted the TTEAMS training on December 7–8, 2009. Attendees from the Mississippi Band of Choctaw Indians included community members and representatives from its family and community services, public safety, wildlife and parks, courts, and victim services.

Training attendees identified several community issues—alcohol and substance abuse, domestic violence, child abuse, high burglary rate, and victimization of tribal members by other tribal members—for which they wanted to develop strategies to enhance interagency collaboration.

Strategy to Enhance Collaboration

As a result of the training, the Choctaw Department of Public Safety devised a strategy to address these community and public safety issues within the Choctaw communities:

1. **Enhance information sharing.**
    a. Determine issues that require an exchange of interagency data.
    b. Identify interagency contacts and resources necessary for implementation.
    c. Create a focus group of key stakeholders to resolve concerns for successful implementation of the strategy.
    d. Develop a process for evaluation and revision.

2. **Develop interagency partnerships.**
    a. Identify key issues surrounding child abuse, sexual assault, and domestic violence.
    b. Identify key partners who have a vested interest in these key issues.
    c. Hold a stakeholder meeting to develop and discuss interagency cooperation and available resources.

3. **Build community trust.**
    a. Identify potential reasons why community members do not trust law enforcement.
    b. Develop community outreach efforts accordingly.

. . . .
50. "History," Mississippi Band of Choctaw Indians, 2011, www.choctaw.org/aboutMBCI/history/index.html.
51. Ibid.

Outcomes to Date

1. **Enhance information sharing.**

   The Choctaw Department of Public Safety conducted outreach efforts with the tribe's Court Services, Office of the Attorney General, Natural Resources Division, Behavioral Health Center, cultural programs, social services, and community organizations to identify ways to enhance interdepartmental information sharing. These departments now share crime data on key community safety issues such as alcohol and substance abuse, domestic violence, child abuse, and burglary and theft.

   For example, before the public safety department first transports an inmate to the detention facility, which has a 116-bed capacity, the inmate is brought to the hospital for medical clearance and then to the Behavioral Health Center to identify any mental health issues. Based on the diagnosis, either the public safety department brings the inmate to the detention facility, or the inmate remains at the health center, which has an 18-bed capacity, thus helping to reduce the detention facility's large inmate population. Furthermore, the department provided the Behavioral Health Center with statistical information for a 30-day period and plans to continue doing this on a regular basis. The department also provides data to other departments and programs for them to include in their grants and reports.

2. **Develop interagency partnerships.**

   Developed under a grant program, a multidisciplinary team consisting of key stakeholders focuses on effective case management for child abuse and sexual assault cases. Officers from the Choctaw Department of Public Safety are part of the team.

   The tribe also formed a Domestic Violence Committee that includes representatives from law enforcement, the health center, the tribal council, tribal administration, social services, education, and the Office of the Attorney General. During committee meetings, cases are evaluated for certain factors, including how many children the family unit has, whether the children reside in the household, and if the offender is a repeat offender. Based on the findings, the committee makes recommendations for the wellbeing of the family: e.g., if the child should be removed from the home.

   The Domestic Violence Committee reestablished a domestic violence shelter, and the community celebrated with a grand opening and ribbon cutting ceremony. Prior to the reopening, services were not available on the reservation; victims had to move out of their homes and relocate. The shelter allows victims to stay on the reservation, close to other family members and their support systems.

   In response to the Tribal Law and Order Act of 2010, the community voted on and the tribe passed a resolution to increase fines and sentencing to address domestic violence. The tribe will develop a domestic violence task force to complement services that are presently available.

   The Office of the Attorney General and the Choctaw Department of Public Safety, as a result of interagency partnerships, are working together to investigate referrals on vulnerable adults. For example, an officer may make a referral or a community member could make a recommendation at social services.

In addition, public safety department representatives became members of advisory boards and committees to help fulfill other departments' goals and objectives. Examples of these advisory boards and committees include the Vulnerable Adult Committee, Child Advocacy Group, Committee on Tribal Code Revision, Adult and Youth Drug Courts, Election Board Committee, and Emergency Management. Law enforcement and social services also hold joint protocol meetings to discuss current concerns.

Other collaborative efforts include the public safety department providing information booths at community events organized by other departments, assisting the Behavioral Health Center with its "sticker shock" program to fight underage drinking, assisting the Family Violence and Victim's Services with its after-school events, and seeking programs to educate jail inmates on social ills and healing methods.

3. **Build community trust.**

    Despite not being fully staffed, the public safety department assigned at least one patrol officer to each community, allowing it to be actively involved in all eight communities. As a result of the new assignments, the officers were able to establish relationships with residents and build trust. Officers assigned to the communities also participate in community activities, such as helping the pre-kindergarten booster club with its fundraiser, which includes a carnival and bingo; leading community service efforts with inmates; and helping with tribal funerals and wakes.

    The public safety department is working to build trust with youths by participating in events such as the end-of-the-school-year pow wow. The department's captain serves as the master of ceremonies, and two or three officers participate in the drum group. Two officers also serve as representatives on the Healing to Wellness Committee, which works with the Cultural Affairs Program to hold workshops on the explanation of the history of social dancing, survival skills, healing practices, and traditional storytelling. The Healing to Wellness Committee also holds sweat lodges for program graduates. Graduation is an important honor, and the public safety department ensures officers are present for it.

    Public safety department staff attends community development club meetings and visits schools to provide information about law enforcement. Some officers are also coaches for local youth recreation leagues. In addition, the department co-sponsors a "Toys for Tots" basketball event held before Christmas. The officers, administration staff, and security guards play in the game, serve as concessioners, and assist with cleanup.

    As a result of these efforts, the community and its youths are more interactive with and accepting of the police. For example, youths will choose to sit next to officers at basketball games and talk about the pow wow. One youth even requested information about becoming a police officer. These efforts have resulted in community members being not only more involved but also more vocal about weeding out crime and disorder.

    The public safety department has decreased its overall response time to calls for service since implementing strategies to enhance communication and collaboration.

Another way the public safety department wished to build community trust was by incorporating culture and traditions into outreach efforts. For example:

- Captain Harold Comby was honored to participate in an elder group discussion to promote tourism in a culturally sensitive way at the sacred historical Choctaw mound from which, according to legend, the tribe's people originated.

- The Choctaw Detention Facility provides community service workers for cultural events, funeral wakes, and services such as yard cleaning for elders. Recently, a couple of inmates helped dig a grave for a deceased tribal member to help grant the wishes of the family that wanted a traditional burial.

- The public safety department assisted the Natural Resources Division in conducting "Stewardship of Nature" for the community by helping to stock ponds and lakes for fishing rodeos. The director of the Wildlife and Parks Program, also the tribal biologist, brings live animals to and provides presentations about wildlife at the schools and tribal-sponsored events.

Lessons Learned

It takes time for the community to develop trust with police. Don't lie to the people; they always can tell when someone is lying. Police departments must remember to follow through on its word by calling people back and following up on issues it said it would look into.

Additional Community Policing Activities

The Choctaw Department of Public Safety has implemented additional community policing activities, including making presentations at the community churches, using equine therapy with at-risk youth, and establishing a wellness garden.

The department has also developed strong working relationships with the three major adjacent parishes (i.e., counties) and nearby cities.

The community is becoming more focused on its culture, with 53 percent of the membership speaking the First Language. More individuals are undergoing traditional naming ceremonies,[52] and the band's relationship to the horse culture is growing.

Contact Information

Choctaw Department of Public Safety
125 River Ridge Circle
Choctaw, MS 39350
Ph: 601-663-7637
Fax: 601-663-7635

Lead Contacts

Wendell Willis, Director of Public Safety | wwillis@choctaw.org

Harold Comby, Captain | hcomby@choctaw.org

Lead Agency Demographics

The Choctaw Department of Public Safety consists of the Choctaw Police Department, Choctaw Detention Facility, the Wildlife and Parks Program, and the Animal Control Program. The employees enforce tribal, state, and federal law on their reservation lands.

. . . .

52. According to Harold Comby, captain of the Choctaw Department of Public Safety, traditional naming ceremonies occur at birth and when a tribal member reaches adulthood. The name given during the first ceremony could be related to a significant event; e.g., if it is raining when a tribal member is born, he or she could be named "Ohmba chi," which means rainmaker. In adulthood, the name may be based on the man or woman's personality. Traditionally, for a man, the naming ceremony would take place when he distinguishes himself in battle. The naming ceremony is the traditional way, but now most tribal members keep their original name until they die.

▲ *The traditions, history, and culture of a tribe play a significant role in the design of any tribal community policing program.*

The Choctaw Police Department formed in 1968 and was a Bureau of Indian Affairs agency until 1985. Presently, the department consists of 54 sworn officers, 31 security officers, four wildlife officers, 47 detention officers and one animal control officer.

Mission Statement

"The mission of the Law Enforcement Services Program is to protect and serve the people who reside or visit the tribe's communities through a comprehensive public safety program which provides both law enforcement and detention services."[53]

. . . .

53. Harold Comby, "Choctaw Department of Public Safety Mission Statement" (presented to Fox Valley Technical College, Appleton, WI, March 7, 2013).

Coquille Indian Tribe

About the Tribe

The Coquille Indian Tribe is headquartered in the Coos Bay and North Bend cities on Oregon's southern coast.[54] Although a treaty negotiated in 1855 acknowledged Indian title to the Coquille lands, the U.S. Congress never ratified it.[55] Many Coquille members returned to their homelands and fought for Congress to acknowledge this treaty, and in 1989 Congress restored the tribe to federal recognition and gave tribal sovereignty.[56] The tribe has more than 968 enrolled members, 506 of whom reside in the tribe's five-county service area.[57]

Website: www.coquilletribe.org

Overview

The Coquille tribal community hosted the TTEAMS training on November 29–30, 2010. Attendees from the Coquille Indian Tribe included representatives from its law enforcement department, courts, and housing authority. In addition, representatives from the Coos County Juvenile Department and the Confederated Tribes of Coos, Lower Umpqua, and Suislaw Indians Police Department were also in attendance.

Attendees identified high rates of juvenile crime as the tribal community's main public safety concern. These crimes, including alcohol and substance abuse and other delinquent behavior such as theft, occurred after school hours and during the summer. The Coquille Tribal Police Department felt that the youths' delinquent behaviors resulted from boredom and lack of parental supervision. The age group most involved in criminal activity was youths in elementary school up to sixth grade. The Coquille Tribal Police Department wanted to use the TTEAMS training concepts to address this high rate of juvenile crime.

Strategy to Address Juvenile Crime

The Coquille Tribal Police Department identified the following strategies to address juvenile crime rates:

1. **Implement a referral process for juveniles engaged in delinquent behavior.**
   a. Identify available services within the tribal community.
   b. Identify non-tribal city, state, and federal agency resources that the tribe can use if necessary.
   c. Work with service providers to identify root causes of particular behaviors, and provide referrals accordingly.

2. **Identify activities through which officers can become more involved with youths.**
   a. Identify activities, and assign specific duties as part of officers' patrol shifts.

3. **Develop an informal reporting process for youths to share information with law enforcement.**
   a. Build youths' trust in law enforcement so they feel comfortable in reporting criminal activity/delinquent behavior.
   b. Identify a response plan.
   c. Create a process to ensure and maintain confidentiality.

. . . .

54. Velarde Tiller, Tiller's Guide to Indian Country, 887.

55. "Culture," Coquille Indian Tribe, 2013, www.coquilletribe.org/Culture.html.

56. Ibid.

57. "About us the Coquille Tribe Overview," Coquille Indian Tribe, 2013, www.coquilletribe.org/AboutUs.html.

4. **Form a youth committee under the direction of the tribal Community Center to organize activities for youths.**

   a. Identify key stakeholders.

   b. Determine the focus of youth committee.

   c. Establish committee goals.

   d. Determine meeting schedule/location/time(s).

5. **Incorporate established K-9 program in schools to help address youth alcohol and substance abuse issues.**

   a. Identify participating schools, and establish collaborative efforts between the schools and law enforcement.

   b. Maintain a routine schedule for visits / locker checks.

Outcomes to Date

1. **Implement a referral process for juveniles engaged in delinquent behavior.**

   When youths are involved in criminal acts, the Coquille Tribal Police Department refers them to the tribal court system, which works closely with other tribal service providers, such as social services, the Community Center, and the Community Health Center.

   Referrals for services may include counseling, anger management classes, parenting classes for and about delinquent youths, and involvement in a tribal healing process, which involves cultural events led by elders who volunteer their time. These cultural events include clam digging, berry picking, and youths helping with scheduled tribal events.

   As part of the healing process, the parties involved in delinquent behavior participate in a healing circle to talk about what occurred. The healing circles help youths build new skills and understand how their behavior affects others. These efforts also attempt to get at the root causes of the youth's behavior rather than treating just the symptoms. For example, if a single, working parent thinks he or she has no other option but to leave the children unsupervised, the program provides the parent with appropriate resources to assist with childcare and supervision.

2. **Identify activities through which officers can become more involved with youths.**

   The Coquille Tribal Police Department created several opportunities that allow officers to become more involved with youths:

   - **Foot and bike patrol:** The police department increased foot and bike patrols during after-school hours and in the summer. Youths are excited to see an officer in their neighborhood and frequently run out to greet them.

   - **Bike rodeo:** The tribe hosts an annual bike rodeo that typically draws 30 youths who learn about bike safety and become familiar with the bike trails. A state-certified bike patrol officer who is on staff at the police department leads the rodeo.

- **Regularly scheduled visits:** As part of their shift management responsibilities, officers routinely schedule time to visit the five neighboring schools in Coos Bay and North Bend, after-school programs, the daycare center, the Community Center, the Community Health Center, and other popular youth venues. During visits to the Community Center, officers are able to interact with youths during open gym and while they are playing on the playground or working on computers. The Community Center also offers a teen group meeting, summer school/academy program, and snow camp, all of which the officers visit. Officers also visit the Head Start program for 3–5 year olds and read to the children. The ultimate goal of the visits is to reach out to youth at an early age and begin building trust.
- **Presentations:** When requested, the police department provides presentations at the school and at parent/teacher nights. One presentation included a discussion on texting and Internet-related crimes.
- **Game night:** The police department participates in game night, which includes basketball games, to encourage positive interactions with families.
- **Fishing derby:** The police department participates in an annual fishing derby for youths and their parents as an opportunity to interact with community members and visitors. Winners of the derby receive prizes.

The Coquille Tribal Police Department has noted that when youths participate in after-school and other tribal programs together with the officers, some underlying causes of delinquent behavior—boredom, the opportunity to participate in delinquent behavior, and a lack of supervision—are eliminated. As a result, the police department noted a decline in delinquent behavior.

As a result of participating in these activities, the youths had the opportunity to interact with law enforcement on a personal level, making youths feel more comfortable reporting unlawful activities.

3. **Develop an informal reporting process for youths to share information with law enforcement.**

Many youths within the community recognize the harm caused by other youths who commit crimes and subject themselves and others to substance abuse. Youths are coming forward to share information with officers about delinquent behaviors witnessed in the community. This is happening because the officers' participation in youth programs and activities has made youths feel more comfortable speaking with officers. Some of the trust lies in the fact that officers maintain confidentiality in their reports and anonymity about the youths providing the tips. These youths not only can report information to the officers but also can contact the police department's dispatch center.

Once law enforcement receives reports from the youths, the police department refers delinquent youths to the appropriate services based on the identified need. Case workers at the Community Health Center handle most cases and then report back to law enforcement about the youth's progress and whether any further law enforcement action is required.

4. **Form a youth committee under the direction of the tribal Community Center to organize activities for youths.**

The tribe formed a youth committee to represent youths who are 12–18 years of age. The tribe has a Teen Night at the community center with safe, drug-free activities.

5. **Incorporate established K-9 program in schools to help address youth alcohol and substance abuse issues.**

    The police department acquired a drug dog for general patrol and seeking out illegal drugs in the community. The tribal council initially approved funds for the dog; the Bureau of Indian Affairs later reimbursed the tribe. In October 2012, the police department expanded the K-9 program to work in all tribal departments and in the community. The K-9 officer and his K-9 partner go into the high schools and complete routine locker checks. The housing office also requested the K-9 officers conduct residence checks when residents leave the housing facilities. This program helped to develop a rapport with both youths and the community, and everyone is now aware that law enforcement is actively working to keep alcohol and substance abuse issues out of the school environment.

While no current statistics are available, the Coquille Tribal Police Department noted a decline in juvenile criminal activity. They also noticed positive behavioral changes in certain youths as a result of the implemented strategies.

Lessons Learned

To implement successful community policing programs, a police department must build trust and rapport with the community as a whole. Officers must be visible and accessible and step outside of the patrol car to interact with individuals, whether that's through foot and bike patrols, visiting community centers and schools, or participating in community events and activities.

Additional Community Policing Activities

The Coquille Tribal Police Department has begun a pilot reserve officer program in which two college students exploring careers in law enforcement are current participants. They're able to go on ride-alongs with officers and experience daily duties such as report writing. Although the program runs primarily during the summer months while the students are on break, the program has received extremely positive feedback from the Tribal Council and the community.

The police department also offers child car seats to tribal members and provides assistance with the installation.

It also created a substation within its office for the Coos County Sheriff's Office. The deputies utilize the substation to work with tribal law enforcement officers, meet with tribal members, and write reports, promoting a positive experience and interaction between community members and the deputies.

The Coquille Indian Housing Authority, which oversees 50–70 homes in the area, requires occupants to sign an Agreement of Conditions and strictly enforces a code of conduct for all household members. This agreement reinforces positive behavior within the housing community.

The police department has also developed working relationships with surrounding tribal communities and local departments and can provide resources to assist these other agencies, especially those negatively impacted by budget cuts. The police department has six memoranda of understanding (MOUs) in place with other agencies and is in the process of developing additional MOUs.

Contact Information

Coquille Tribal Police Department
3050 Tremont Street
North Bend, OR 97459
Ph: 541-888-0189
Fax: 541-888-2239

Lead Contact

Scott LaFevre, Chief of Police | cipolice@coquilletribe.org

Lead Agency Demographics

The police department employs a chief of police and three officers and has a patrol area approximately 10 miles long with an additional 5,900 acres in the Coquille Forest.[58] The department does not employ any office or civilian staff. All officers are duly sworn as deputy sheriffs with the Coos County Sheriff's Office; they have the same powers as a deputy sheriff to enforce state criminal and traffic laws on and off tribal property.

Mission Statement

"The mission of the Coquille Tribal Police Department is "to provide service, safety, and security to tribal members and visitors." [59]

58. "Coquille Tribal Police Welcome," Coquille Indian Tribe, 2013,
    www.coquilletribe.org/coquille-indian-tribe-police.htm.

59. Coquille Tribal Police Department, "Mission Statement" (presented to Fox Valley Technical College, Appleton, WI,
    November 30, 2012).

Shoalwater Bay Indian Tribe

About the Tribe

The Shoalwater Bay Indian Reservation is located near Tokeland on the Willapa Bay on the western shore of the state of Washington. The tribe, formed in 1866 and officially recognized in 1971, incorporates members of Lower Chehalis, Shoalwater Bay, and the Chinookan people. The Shoalwater Bay Indian Tribe is located on 355 acres of land and has more than 300 enrolled members. The tribe has a strong culture and heritage, and many of the tribe's members still hold true to traditional spiritual beliefs and practices.

Website: www.shoalwaterbay-nsn.gov

Overview

The Shoalwater Bay Indian Tribe hosted the TTEAMS training in Tokeland, Washington, on December 2–3, 2010. Attendees from the Shoalwater Bay Indian Tribe included community members and representatives from treatment and health services, education, law enforcement, tribal administration, and emergency management. The tribe focused its community policing efforts on enhancing relationships between law enforcement and the community, in particular the youths, to address alcohol and substance abuse. Although the reservation is approximately one square mile in size, drugs, particularly meth, heroin, and prescription medications, continue to be a concern for the safety of the community.

Strategy to Enhance Relationships with Youths and the Community

As a result of the training, the Shoalwater Bay Police Department identified a plan to develop an after-school youth program to improve relationships and build trust between law enforcement and youths. The department identified the following key steps:

1. **Implement youth programs.**
   a. Meet with the tribal council.
   b. Meet with school administrators.
   c. Share the schedule of after-school activities with law enforcement.
   d. Assign an on-duty officer to visit the after-school program, participate in activities, and interact with youths.

Outcomes to Date

Over the past year, progress in implementing the strategy has been gradual because of a high turnover rate at the police department. However, the department recently hired new officers, and momentum is building; even with the current challenge, there has been great success.

1. **Implement youth programs.**

   The after-school programs are open to all local tribal youths. As part of the programs, an on-duty officer visits and interacts with the youths. During the visits, the officer participates in scheduled after-school activities such as homework sessions. Youths now look for and ask for the visiting officers.

   The Shoalwater police officers also participated in the "Shop with a Cop" program with two youths from the after-school program. Through the program, youth participate in a ride-along with an officer. In addition, the program provides the youth with a stipend to go holiday shopping and gives them holiday food items for their family.

To continue reaching out to youths during the summer, the police department coordinates an annual bike rodeo that brings youths together to learn about bike safety. During the event, youths participate in a safety course on using protective bike gear and hand signals, and they receive brochures on bike safety. They also have an opportunity to participate in a raffle for prizes such as bikes and helmets.

Youth programs will continue to grow as the police department hires additional officers.

Additional Community Policing Activities

The Shoalwater Bay Tribe has been successful in its community policing activities. Future community policing goals include developing neighborhood watch groups.

Lessons Learned

Change does not happen in one day. It can take a lot of time to see even a small change. It is important for law enforcement to show its dedication to the program. Showing dedication helps build community trust.

Contact Information

Shoalwater Bay Police Department
PO Box 130
Tokeland, WA 98590
Ph: 360-267-8195

Lead Contact

Robin Souvenir, Chief of Police | rsouvenir@shoalwaterbay-nsn.gov

Lead Agency Demographics

The Shoalwater Bay Police Department protects and serves the community.[60] The service area is approximately one square mile in size and is located on a peninsula. The department comprises the chief of police, patrol sergeant, and three officers.

Mission Statement

"The Shoalwater Bay Police Department values integrity, dedication and loyalty. Through professionalism and discipline we strive to meet the highest standards of law enforcement service and community policing. With patience and understanding we aim to protect and serve the Shoalwater Bay Indian Nation and further the combined goals of the Department and the community on a day to day basis."[61]

. . . .

60. "Shoalwater Services: Public Safety—Police," Shoalwater Bay Tribe, 2013, www.shoalwaterbay-nsn.gov/home/shoalwater-services/public-safety/.

61. Ibid.

Washoe Tribe of Nevada and California
About the Tribe

The Washoe Tribe has approximately 3,500 acres of land located in Nevada and California.[62] Its history goes back an estimated 9,000 years,[63] and the tribe's members "are the original inhabitants of 'Da ow aga' (Lake Tahoe) and all the lands surrounding it."[64] Lake Tahoe remains the center of the Washoe culture; in addition to the lake, the landscape of the reservation encompasses mountain forests, alpine meadows, and Pinion-juniper woodlands.[65] The Washoe language dialect is Hokan, which is distinctive to the tribe.[66]

The Washoe Tribe "has four communities with three located in Nevada (Stewart, Carson, and Dresslerville) and one in California (Woodfords)."[67] The tribe has jurisdiction over trust allotments in both states, with additional tribal trust parcels in Alpine, Placer, Sierra, Douglas, Carson, and Washoe Counties.[68] A tribal council and chairwoman/chairman govern the tribe.

Website: www.washoetribe.us/home.html

Overview

The Washoe Tribe hosted the TTEAMS training on August 4–5, 2011. Attendees from the Washoe Tribe included community members and representatives from various agencies and disciplines, including law enforcement, corrections, tribal administration, health, social services, education, and housing. Throughout the training, attendees learned about community oriented policing strategies and how to develop partnerships to implement these strategies to address community challenges. The training team identified one main goal: youth outreach to address and prevent delinquent behaviors.

The Washoe Tribal Police Department and community indicated there was a high volume of youths involved in underage drinking and partying, marking or tagging with graffiti, and truancy. Following the training, the Washoe tribal community and police department wanted to explore methods to involve community members in identifying youth outreach activities.

. . . .

62. "Washoe Tribal Court," California Courts, last modified 2013, www.courts.ca.gov/14798.htm.
63. "History and Culture," Washoe Tribe of Nevada and California, last modified 2010, www.washoetribe.us/history-a-culture.html.
64. Lissa Guimaraes Dodds, "Wa She Shu: 'The Washoe People' Past and Present" (The Washoe Tribe of Nevada and California, Washoe Cultural Resource Office, 2009), 5.
65. "Washoe Tribe of Nevada and California," last modified 2010, www.washoetribe.us/history-a-culture.html.
66. Ibid.
67. "History and Culture," Washoe Tribe of Nevada and California, last modified 2010, www.washoetribe.us/history-a-culture.html.
68. Ibid.

Strategy to Address Juvenile Delinquency

As a result of the training, attendees identified a strategy to engage the community in developing youth activities and outreach. To accomplish outreach efforts, the Washoe Tribal Police Department identified the following action steps and activities while ensuring the four Washoe communities were equally involved:

1. **Implement quarterly meetings.**
   a. Identify meeting locations, and schedule quarterly meetings, rotating between the four communities.
   b. Conduct a survey in each community to learn more about community members.
   c. Share the meeting location, date, and time with community members.
   d. Identify methods to gain community interest and attendance.
   e. Identify meeting agenda items.
   f. Conduct meetings.

2. **Host a youth awareness day.**
   a. Identify a location for the activity and a rotation schedule among the four communities.
   b. Identify potential activities and public safety presentations.
   c. Share youth awareness day information with the communities.
   d. Survey youths.

3. **Provide youth safety classes.**
   a. Contact local Head Start programs to introduce classes.
   b. Schedule time to conduct youth safety classes.

4. **Identify positive role models to work with youths.**
   a. Identify activities to bring law enforcement and youths together.
   b. Schedule and hold activities.

5. **Hold a youth event.**
   a. Identify partner agencies.
   b. Identify training topics and activities that will assist youths in making positive life choices.
   c. Schedule and conduct the event.

6. **Employ a youth probation officer.**
   a. Define roles and responsibilities for the position.
   b. Identify service population, including at-risk youths not yet involved in the judicial system.
   c. Have both the youth and adult probation officers report to the police department, as the tribal court judge is a part-time, contract employee.

Outcomes to Date

The Washoe Tribe was successful in implementing youth outreach activities. To date, each of the key action steps and activities has reflected progress.

1. **Implement quarterly meetings.**

   The Washoe Tribal Police Department implemented quarterly community meetings. In the nine months following the training, the police department conducted three community meetings that rotated among the communities it serves, and approximately 30 community members attended each meeting. To create a more comfortable atmosphere and encourage attendees to engage in conversation, the police department began providing food and refreshments during meetings, which seems to have improved attendance. Also, the department asks attendees to complete a survey to help law enforcement gain more insight about the community members it serves.

   During the meetings, the police department provides an overview of its activities and time to discuss community concerns. For example, a meeting held in May 2012 discussed safety concerns over abandoned trailers and large sage growths that were serving as hiding spots for youths and adults, especially at night. The community members recommended that the trailers, which were also used as party houses, be removed and the large sage growths be cut down. The police department worked with the Community Council and the Tribal Environmental Department to remove five of the trailers and is working with community leaders to have the sagebrush removed in the near future. Other safety topics discussed included home safety. The police department recommended that community members consider installing motion lighting to help alert each other of possible suspicious activities.

   Following each quarterly meeting, the police department distributes a survey to the meeting attendees, offering them an opportunity to make recommendations and suggest topics for the next quarterly meeting. Since the police department implemented the community meetings, participation at the meetings and overall community involvement continue to increase.

2. **Host a youth awareness day.**

   The police department sponsored a youth engagement and awareness day, and those who attended were between the ages of four and 18. Activities included public safety presentations, simulations on the dangers of impaired driving using distortion goggles and a motorized cart, a bounce house, music, a barbeque, and a raffle. The department asked those attending to complete an evaluation of the day's events; as a result, the department is considering whether to host the awareness day annually, rotating each year among the four communities.

3. **Provide youth safety classes.**

   The police department is working with local Head Start programs to offer safety classes to youths enrolled in the program. Classes typically last 30 minutes and include "Stranger-Danger," "Stop, Drop, and Roll" fire safety, responding to dangerous situations for children, and other aspects of safety, all based on current events and staff demands.

4. **Identify positive role models to work with youths.**

   The Washoe Tribe Police Department coordinated a number of activities to help connect youths with positive role models:

   - **Halloween treats:** Police officers went in to the communities with bags of candy that contained anti-drug messages and stickers. Officers distributed between 250 and 300 bags of candy to the youths. The department will continue to distribute police badge stickers throughout the year.
   - **Law Enforcement Memorial Run:** The Washoe Tribe was the only Native American community in Nevada that had a statewide memorial run take place in its community. Community members cheered the runners along the route.
   - **Basketball games:** To show community support, the police department sends officers to community basketball games involving youths and adults. There was even a game between community members and police department employees.

5. **Hold a youth event.**

   The Washoe Tribe is partnering with two other tribal communities, the Yerington Paiute Tribe and the Walker River Paiute Tribe, to plan a youth event that will span two and a half days. The event will focus on providing information about making good decisions and the possible consequences of making bad decisions. Youth sessions will discuss bullying, harassment, and cultural traditions such as beading and hand games. Non-uniformed tribal police officers will serve as youth mentors. Other activities will include a youth dance. The tribe hopes that this interaction with young children will show them a path to a better lifestyle by making good decisions.

6. **Employ a youth probation officer.**

   The Washoe Tribe funded a tribal youth probation officer position that entails working with children adjudicated by the court and with other at-risk youths. The probation officer will incorporate cultural activities into the program and will establish memoranda of agreement with other tribal youth service providers. The cultural component includes taking a language class and talking with specific, respected elders about how youths acted in the past. Adding the youth probation officer position gave the current probation officer the opportunity to focus solely on adults. Both of the tribe's probation officers report to the police department because the tribal court judge is a part-time, contract employee.

Lessons Learned

As a result of the activities implemented, the overall crime rate is trending down. Calls for service declined by 10 percent, and the number of cases dropped. The Washoe Tribe Police Department also noticed that community members now offer more information to the police when calling for assistance. In addition, citizens are placing more calls before a crime occurs. The police department has ambitious plans for the near future, noting the need to expand current programs and develop new programs. It hopes to establish a youth cadet program, similar to a police explorer program, and an overnight camp for youths.

Additional Community Policing Activities

In addition to Washoe Tribe's strategies to address juvenile delinquency in the community, it has implemented additional community policing programs:

- **Elder checks:** The police department identified the need to conduct elder safety checks at least once a month; to date, the department has identified between 40 and 50 tribal elders. The officers who conduct the checks prepare monthly reports and provide them to the chief of police. If the officer conducting the elder safety check determines the elder needs assistance or a service, the officer will contact the Washoe Tribe Social Services Department to provide a referral. The police department and social services department will then work together to ensure the elder receives the assistance needed.

  The police department preforms elder safety checks out of respect for the elders and to identify what their needs might be during emergencies. For example, during an electrical outage, law enforcement and EMS know which elders rely on electricity for medical life-saving devices. In return, elders have the opportunity to be involved in the safety and wellbeing of the community by providing officers with cultural insight and historical perspectives of the tribal community as a whole.

- **Charity drives:** To enhance its rapport with the community, the police department organizes charity drives for winter coats and food. Prior to the winter of 2011, the department helped collect more than 200 coats and distributed them in the four communities as needed. It also collected food items and distributed turkey meals to 40 families over the Thanksgiving holiday.

- **Interacting with other departments:** Law enforcement also provided training to the Washoe Housing Authority on drug use recognition, mandatory reporting laws for child abuse, and other community safety issues. The housing authority closed for the training so all staff had the opportunity to participate.

Contact Information

Washoe Tribal Police Department
950 Highway 395 South
Gardnerville, NV 89410
Ph: 775-265-7540 (office)
Fax: 775-265-2508

Lead Contacts

Richard Varner, Chief of Police | richard.varner@washoetribe.us

John Leonard, Sergeant | john.leonard@washoetribe.us

Lead Agency Demographics

The Washoe Tribe Police Department consists of nine sworn positions and one civilian position. It contracts with one local county for dispatch and 911 services and with another county for detention needs. The police department has jurisdiction in four communities.

Mission Statement

"It is the mission of the Washoe Tribe Police Department is to safeguard the lives and property of the people we serve, to reduce the incidence and fear of crime, and to enhance public safety while working with the Washoe Communities to improve their quality of life. Our mandate is to perform with honor and integrity by conducting ourselves with the highest ethical standards." [69]

. . . .

69. "Washoe Tribe of Nevada & California Law Enforcement," Washoe Tribe of Nevada & California, last modified 2010, www.washoetribe.us/administration/programsdepartments/law-enforcement.html.

Kalispel Tribe

The Kalispel Indian Reservation is located in Pend Oreille County, Washington, approximately 55 miles north of Spokane.[70] The main reservation, known as the north reservation, has 4,654 acres located along the Pend Oreille River's east bank near Usk, Washington, with an additional 240 acres along the west bank of the river.[71] In 1996, the tribe obtained ownership of approximately 300 acres in Airway Heights, known as the south reservation, which houses a casino and resort hotel.[72] About one-third of the tribe's 400 enrolled members reside on the reservation.[73]

Website: www.kalispeltribe.com/kalispel-tribal-public-safety-department

Overview

The Kalispel Tribe hosted the TTEAMS training on April 26–27, 2010. Those in attendance from the Kalispel Tribe represented various agencies and disciplines, including law enforcement, behavioral health, health services, children and family services, domestic violence, the substance abuse program, and the courts and legal department. Also in attendance were social services from the Coeur D'Alene Tribe and law enforcement from the Confederated Tribes of the Colville Reservation. Other attendees included representatives from the Washington State Department of Corrections; Pend Oreille County counseling services, victim services, emergency management, and law enforcement; Rural Resources Community Action; and Stevens County Substance Abuse Coalition.

Because the tribe is located on two sites, the Kalispel Tribal Public Safety Department must serve a split jurisdiction with limited staff. As such, several ideas and some specific issues emerged from the training, such as the need for enhancing collaboration and developing creative solutions to address crime trends. Specifically, the attendees identified and discussed two main issues: possible prostitution activities on the casino property and prescription drug abuse in the tribal community.

Regarding the casino, its resort hotel staff and tribal police officers began to notice possible illegal activities at the property, which is located 60 miles away from the north reservation. Unfortunately, Kalispel police officers were unable to enforce the law adequately because they lacked jurisdiction over non-Natives; approximately 7,000 to 10,000 people visit the 250-room resort hotel daily. The police officers conducted an investigation and found that some females were advertising their services at the hotel with pictures of them in rooms distinctive to the tribal resort. As the investigation continued, some of the females agreed to become confidential informants and ultimately indicated they advertised their services on public websites and on a restricted-membership website controlled by one individual. Furthermore, a large percentage of these females were dependent on drugs, and prostitution supported their drug habit.

The attendees determined that the police also needed to address the second issue, prescription drug abuse, because the tribal community had lost three members from prescription drug overdoses over a three-year period. The police also noticed the trend of abusing prescription drugs among community members. Some young people were stealing prescription drugs from parents, grandparents, or acquaintances and selling them.

. . . .

70. "Our Land," Kalispel Tribe of Indians, 2009, www.kalispeltribe.com/our-land/.

71. Ibid.

72. Ibid.

73. "About Us," Kalispel Tribe of Indians, 2009, www.kalispeltribe.com/about-us/.

Strategy to Address Crime

The Kalispel Tribal Public Safety Department identified the following strategies to address prostitution activities and prescription drug abuse:

1. **Enhance collaboration between tribal and nontribal law enforcement groups due to limited tribal police presence at the casino and hotel.**

   a. Complete state law enforcement academy certification for all Kalispel tribal police officers.

      i. Identify collaborating agencies, and develop a process to complete the memorandum of understanding between the Airway Heights Police Department and the Pend Oreille County Sheriff's Office.

      ii. Complete the memorandum of understanding and the memorandum of agreement by July 2013.

   b. Identify and prioritize problems and resources that can be used to develop strategies across agencies and jurisdictions.

2. **Develop a working group to address prostitution, money laundering, drug trafficking, and human trafficking.**

   a. Invite departments and agencies to participate in the first meeting.

   b. Identify goals and objectives.

   c. Determine methods that prostitutes are using to solicit.

   d. Review surveillance footage, collect evidence, interview confidential informants, and document and review findings.

   e. Set regular meetings to discuss progress and future direction. This should include a meeting between a team of officers and the superior court judge to seal the record while law enforcement collects search warrants, subpoenas, and investigation materials.

3. **Hold community oriented policing meetings at the reservation.**

   a. Set a quarterly meeting schedule.

   b. Invite interested parties.

   c. Set meeting agendas based on issues identified at the onset.

   d. Identify methods to collect data that can be available in real time to respond quickly to criminal activities (apply for grant funding if necessary).

   e. Use the scanning, analysis, response, and assessment (SARA)[74] model to identify and prioritize problems, research the dynamics of the problem, implement strategies to address identified problem, and evaluate impact and outcomes.

4. **Form a prescription drug abuse community coalition.**

   a. Schedule the initial meeting, and invite local physicians, dentists, hospital administrators, police, teachers, prevention workers, and community members to participate.

   b. Gather prescription drug data (prescriptions provided and dosages) from pharmacies in Pend Oreille County, and disseminate collected information to members of the coalition.

   c. Have the coalition group identify potential educational efforts, unified protocols, and provisions for community services to bring about changes in prescribing practices.

   d. Help educate patients and the local community about the risks and alternatives to chronic opiate use.

. . . .

74 To learn more about the SARA model, see "What is Community Policing" on page 1.

    e. Track the reduction of prescribed opiates; target a 50 percent reduction within three years.

    f. Order a DEA drop box to be placed in the tribe's Public Safety Building, and identify this and other sites as safe, drop-off locations. (Collaborate with the Pend Oreille county sheriff to target two dates per year to advertise drop-off locations.)

Outcomes to Date

1. **Enhance collaboration between tribal and nontribal law enforcement groups due to limited tribal police presence at the casino and hotel.**

   In conjunction with recent changes in state laws, Kalispel police officers are now eligible to attend the Washington State Police Academy and other specialized trainings to receive state certification and recognition. The Kalispel Tribal Public Safety Department is currently finalizing with the surrounding jurisdictions the memorandum of understanding and the memorandum of agreement that would give it state jurisdiction over non-Natives.

   The tribe is currently working with the academy to incorporate a training segment on recognizing and understanding Native American traditions and cultures. For example, nontribal officers need to recognize items such as sweetgrass and sage that Natives use in traditional ways.

   The tribe also adopted the philosophy of community policing. It wants to be more inclusive and to seek out assistance from community members, using nontraditional approaches such as creating an anonymous tipline, implementing knock and talks (i.e., police making home visits), developing confidential informants, and using community questionnaires and evaluations. Recognizing the need to consider nontraditional approaches has allowed members to suggest new ways to address old problems.

2. **Develop a working group to address prostitution, money laundering, drug trafficking, and human trafficking.**

   To identify possible illegal activities, the Kalispel Tribal Public Safety Department developed a working group that includes representatives from the city of Airway Heights Police Department and the Washington State Gambling Commission. Further investigation revealed that prostitutes were offering their services online and in massage parlors near the city of Spokane.

   For purposes of addressing this particular issue, the initial working group expanded into a larger, organized task force to collaborate on the investigation. In July 2012, 150 officers from 14 agencies and federal departments seized and shut down eight massage parlors and arrested the owners/operators. They seized more than $200,000 in cash along with cars and a house. Racketeering charges included money laundering, drug possession, prostitution, human trafficking, and pandering with minors. The following agencies participated in what is now known as the Red Light Spa Raid:

   - **Tribal**
     - Kalispel Tribal Public Safety Department

   - **County**
     - Grant County Sheriff's Office
     - Spokane County Sheriff's Office

■ **Local**
- — Airway Heights Police Department
- — Cheney Police Department
- — Liberty Lake Police Department
- — City of Spokane Police Department

■ **State**
- — Washington Gambling Commission
- — Washington State Patrol

■ **Federal**
- — Federal Bureau of Investigation
- — Internal Revenue Service
- — U.S. Border Patrol
- — U.S. Department of Homeland Security
- — U.S. Immigration and Customs Enforcement

Since the arrests, the Kalispel Tribal Public Safety Department has continued its efforts in proactively addressing these particular crimes.

Due to the efforts of the working group, the tribe developed a close working relationship with the FBI in Spokane. The public safety department is currently working with the FBI to get its sergeant commissioned, which will give him the ability to assist other tribes without jurisdictional restrictions.

3. **Hold community oriented policing meetings at the reservation.**

The Kalispel Tribal Public Safety Department holds quarterly meetings on the north reservation to discuss community policing issues. The meetings include police, fire departments, and community members, and the public safety department now plans to expand these meetings to include casino and hotel representatives from their south reservation.

The public safety department has identified meeting topics by asking community members for their input. The department's aim is to provide multiple opportunities and as many avenues as possible for community members to respond, if they wish. For example, the department installed an anonymous tip line, enabling it to collect information regarding key community concerns. The meetings discuss topics of concern as requested by community members.

The public safety department promotes the meetings through postcards, hand-delivered notices, and e-mails to tribal employees as well as by talking to people whom the officers encounter while working. In the near future, the department plans to meet with its marketing department to discuss ways to use social media, such as Facebook, to promote meetings and events.

4. **Form a prescription drug abuse community coalition.**

The loss of three tribal members due to prescription drug abuse in a three-year period had a profound impact on the tribal community. A doctor from the tribe's medical clinic contacted the tribe's DOJ COPS Office coordinator to discuss the high number of opiate-addicted members in the community.

In response, the police department's COPS Office meth grant coordinator, a civilian employee, worked with the Kalispel tribal physician to start a community coalition, RX WATCH, to raise awareness and address the dangers of prescription drug abuse. This included meeting with individuals who have the power to change prescribing practices: e.g., physicians, hospital/health clinic staff, pharmacists, dentists, and veterinarians. In addition, the COPS Office meth grant coordinator and Kalispel tribal physician invited interested community members (e.g., prevention groups, law enforcement, treatment providers, members from the education community, and concerned community members) to participate in RX WATCH.

The mission of RX WATCH is to foster collaboration with local health care and other community members to reduce the addiction, family destruction, crime, and death caused by excessive opiate use and its availability. The group defined the following goals:

- Reduce prescribing opiate narcotics by 50 percent within next three years.

- Support providers through educational efforts, unified protocols, and provision of community services to change prescribing practices.

- Gather and disseminate complete and accurate information about the incidence and prevalence of problems associated with opioid misuse.

- Facilitate education about the risks and alternatives of chronic opiate treatment to patients and the local community.

The Kalispel Tribal Police Department's COPS Office meth grant coordinator, as part of RX WATCH, purchased a Drug Enforcement Administration (DEA) drop box. The coordinator schedules and advertises prescription drug drop off events in concert with the national DEA RX drop off dates in an effort to synchronize advertising materials.

The Kalispel Tribal Public Safety Department successfully forged a lasting partnership with the surrounding nontribal police agencies to address identified community issues, and it continues to develop relationships within the community. In addition, the department has sustained its community policing initiatives at the north reservation. Because the tribe has two reservation sites, the department is now a part of strategic meetings that aim to identify ways to incorporate these initiatives at the resort location.

Lessons Learned

Connecting people to resources is important. The Kalispel Tribe's Camas Path program is committed to improving the quality of life for Kalispel tribal and community members and others by addressing the intellectual, emotional, physical, and cultural needs of individuals through education, training, and wellness programs. The tribe encourages law enforcement personnel to give Camas Path Behavioral Health Services' contact information to people who need help addressing drug addiction and other life-altering habits; by doing so, the center can help them become productive persons in the community.

In addition, the RX WATCH coalition was successful in engaging the pharmacy community to collect data and then share that data within the coalition. Because some members of RX WATCH are hospital administrators, physicians, and dentists, they wanted to address overprescribing practices. As a result, the police department and a tribal doctor worked together to gather and share information with the coalition. A physician was able to define safe and dangerous dosage levels. As a result, the hospital hired a pain management physician to begin working with patients who were considered at risk (based on their dosage levels) and to provide those patients with wraparound services to enhance their well-being.

The Kalispel Tribe plans to continue to enhance its community oriented policing efforts by holding regularly scheduled meetings and to begin developing a process at the resort location to engage leadership in the data gathering and sharing crime trends to provide "four star public safety."

Also, the tribe will continue to work on completing a memorandum of understanding between the Airway Heights Police Department and the Pend Oreille County Sheriff's Office with the specifics of "sovereign immunity" spelled out as part of the agreement's standard operating procedure. Each agency needs to understand and respect the other's authority: i.e., when an outside agency needs to enter another agency's jurisdiction, the former should contact the latter to share when it is entering the jurisdiction and for what purpose.

Contact Information

Kalispel Tribal Public Safety Department
PO Box 39
Usk, WA 99180
Ph: 509-447-7124
Fax: 509-481-2107

Lead Contacts

James Wynecoop, Director of Public Safety | jwynecoop@kalispeltribe.com

Rodney Schurger, Sergeant | rshurger@kalispeltribe.com

Lynn Soderquist, DOJ COPS Office Coordinator| lsoderquist@kalispeltribe.com

Lead Agency Demographics

The department consists of 12 sworn positions, including a SORNA officer (SORNA refers to the Sex Offender Registration and Notification Act) and an FBI "Safe Trails" task force officer, and one civilian position.

Mission Statement

"All members of the Kalispel Tribal Public Safety Department will continue to provide professional law enforcement, firefighting and emergency medical services to all members of the Kalispel Community and our neighbors. We are the 'First Line of Defense' against those persons, elements and accidents that may want to harm us or our property."[75]

. . . .

75. "Kalispel Tribal Public Safety Department," Kalispel Tribe of Indians, 2009,
      www.kalispeltribe.com/kalispel-tribal-public-safety-department/.

Conclusion

Since its inception in 1999, the COPS Office's Tribal Resources Grant Program's (TRGP) Tribal Community Police Problem-Solving Teams (TTEAMS) training has provided a foundation for tribal communities to address issues affecting community safety. With an emphasis on sharing the basic concepts of community policing and encouraging the development of problem-solving teams, the training provided opportunities for tribes to build community and interagency relationships to improve community safety. These teams, with an appreciation of each other's roles, identified community concerns and problem-solving approaches to address these concerns effectively.

Many valuable lessons can be gleaned from the tribes discussed in this publication that successfully implemented and continue to implement the TTEAMS process, which highlighted the importance of collaboration and the use of partnerships to develop strategies to improve community safety. For example, Kalispel Tribe used partnerships to help law enforcement connect community members in need of assistance to wellness resources and programs. Another common theme among the tribes was the need to foster open communication and to build trust between law enforcement and community members. For example, the Coquille Tribal Police Department created several activities that allow officers to be more involved with youths, thus creating trust between the police and the community.

▲ During the TTEAMS training hosted by the Makah Tribe in Washington in April 2010, tribal police and community members worked together to identify strategies to address public safety issues in their community.

Since the TTEAMS training first began in Indian Country, it has noticeably changed, as it now involves agencies beyond tribal boundaries. The participation of county sheriffs, municipal police, state police, and representatives of other nontribal agencies at TTEAMS trainings emphasizes the importance of including these agencies when implementing community policing concepts. For example, the Fond Du Lac Band of the Lake Superior Chippewa Tribe enhanced collaboration with the Carlton County Sheriff's Office to address gang issues. This inclusiveness recognizes that crime is mobile and that the success of a tribe's community policing initiatives may depend not only on a tribal police department's relationship with its own community but also on its relationship with nontribal agencies.

The contributions of the tribes herein who have shared their experiences in developing community policing initiatives have provided a comprehensive resource for other tribes wishing to implement community policing programs to improve safety in their communities. Each tribe has provided contact information for individuals interested in seeking more detailed, program information.

The intent of the COPS Office's Tribal Resources Grant Program is to assist tribal law enforcement agencies with implementing or enhancing community policing practices. For more information on TRGP, please contract Matthew Lysakowski, senior advisor for tribal affairs with the U. S. Department of Justice, Office of Community Oriented Policing Services, at 202-514-6392 or matthew.lysakowski@usdoj.gov, or contact the COPS Office Response Center at 800-421-6770 or askCopsRC@usdoj.gov.

Resources

Center for Problem-Oriented Policing. 2013. "The SARA Model." www.popcenter.org/about/?p=sara.

Chitimacha Tribe of Louisiana. 2005. "Genealogy." www.chitimacha.gov/tribal_about_genealogy.htm.

———. 2005. "The Chitimacha Tribal Council." www.chitimacha.gov/tribal_council.htm.

———. 2013. "Chitimacha Tribe of Louisiana – Tribal Government." www.chitimacha.gov/tribal_government.htm.

———. 2005. "History." www.chitimacha.gov/tribal_about_history.htm.

COPS Office. 2012. *Community Policing Defined*. Washington, DC: U.S. Department of Justice, Office of Community Oriented Policing Services. http://ric-zai-inc.com/ric.php?page=detail&id=COPS-P157.

Coquille Indian Tribe. 2013. "About us the Coquille Tribe Overview." www.coquilletribe.org/AboutUs.html.

———. 2013. "Coquille Tribal Police Welcome." www.coquilletribe.org/coquille-indian-tribe-police.htm.

———. 2013. "Culture." www.coquilletribe.org/Culture.html.

Fond du Lac Band of Lake Superior Chippewa. 2013. "FDL Law Enforcement." www.fdlrez.com/police/main.htm.

———. 2013. "Fond du Lac Band of Lake Superior Chippewa." www.fdlrez.com/.

Guimaraes Dodds, Lissa. 2009. "WA SHE SHU: 'The Washoe People' Past and Present." Gardnerville, NV: The Washoe Tribe of Nevada and California, Washoe Cultural Resource Office.

Kalispel Tribe. 2009. "Our Land." www.kalispeltribe.com/our-land/.

———. 2009. "About Us." www.kalispeltribe.com/about-us/.

———. 2009. "Kalispel Tribal Public Safety Department." www.kalispeltribe.com/kalispel-tribal-public-safety-department/.

Lac du Flambeau Band of Lake Superior Chippewa. 2010. "About Us." www.ldftribe.com/about_us.php.

Leech Lake Band of Ojibwe. 2013. "Demographics." www.llojibwe.com.

Maguire, Edward, and Wells, William, eds. 2012. *Implementing Community Policing: Lessons from 12 Agencies*. Washington, D.C.: U.S. Department of Justice, Office of Community Oriented Policing Services.

Menominee Indian Tribe of Wisconsin. 2013. "About Us." www.menominee-nsn.gov/MITW/aboutUs.aspx.

Menominee Tribal Police Department. 2013. "Law Enforcement Center Mission Statement." metp.menominee-nsn.gov.

Mississippi Band of Choctaw Indians. 2011. "History." www.choctaw.org/aboutMBCI/history/index.html.

Oneida Tribe of Indians of Wisconsin. 2013. "About Us." www.oneidanation.org/policedepartment/aboutus.aspx.

———. 2013. "Oneida Tribal Government." www.oneida-nsn.gov.

Pueblo of Isleta. 2013. "Pueblo of Isleta." www.isletapueblo.com.

Puyallup Tribe. 2013. "Puyallup Tribal Police Department Mission Statement." www.puyallup-tribe.com/law-enforcement/puyallup_tribal_police_department/.

———. 2013. "Welcome." www.puyallup-tribe.com.

Shoalwater Bay Indian Tribe. 2013. "Shoalwater Services Public Safety: Police." www.shoalwaterbay-nsn.gov/home/shoalwater-services/public-safety/.

Tonkawa Tribe of Oklahoma. 2013. "Tonkawa Tribal Profile." www.tonkawatribe.com/profile/profile.htm.

Velarde Tiller, Veronica E. 2005. *Tillers Guide to Indian Country*. Albuquerque, NM: Bow Arrow Publishing Company.

Washoe Tribe of Nevada and California. 2010. "Wa She Shu: The Washoe People Past and Present." Last modified 2010. www.washoetribe.us/history-a-culture.html.

———. 2010. "Washoe Tribe of Nevada & California Law Enforcement." Last modified 2010. www.washoetribe.us/administration/programsdepartments/law-enforcement.html.

About the COPS Office

The Office of Community Oriented Policing Services (COPS Office) is the component of the U.S. Department of Justice responsible for advancing the practice of community policing by the nation's state, local, territory, and tribal law enforcement agencies through information and grant resources.

Community policing is a philosophy that promotes organizational strategies that support the systematic use of partnerships and problem-solving techniques, to proactively address the immediate conditions that give rise to public safety issues such as crime, social disorder, and fear of crime.

Rather than simply responding to crimes once they have been committed, community policing concentrates on preventing crime and eliminating the atmosphere of fear it creates. Earning the trust of the community and making those individuals stakeholders in their own safety enables law enforcement to better understand and address both the needs of the community and the factors that contribute to crime.

The COPS Office awards grants to state, local, territory, and tribal law enforcement agencies to hire and train community policing professionals, acquire and deploy cutting-edge crime fighting technologies, and develop and test innovative policing strategies. COPS Office funding also provides training and technical assistance to community members and local government leaders and all levels of law enforcement. The COPS Office has produced and compiled a broad range of information resources that can help law enforcement better address specific crime and operational issues, and help community leaders better understand how to work cooperatively with their law enforcement agency to reduce crime.

- Since 1994, the COPS Office has invested nearly $14 billion to add community policing officers to the nation's streets, enhance crime fighting technology, support crime prevention initiatives, and provide training and technical assistance to help advance community policing.

- By the end of FY2012, the COPS Office has funded approximately 124,000 additional officers to more than 13,000 of the nation's 18,000 law enforcement agencies across the country in small and large jurisdictions alike.

- Nearly 700,000 law enforcement personnel, community members, and government leaders have been trained through COPS Office-funded training organizations.

- As of 2012, the COPS Office has distributed more than 8.5 million topic-specific publications, training curricula, white papers, and resource CDs.

COPS Office resources, covering a wide breadth of community policing topics—from school and campus safety to gang violence—are available, at no cost, through its online Resource Center at www.cops.usdoj.gov. This easy-to-navigate website is also the grant application portal, providing access to online application forms.

About the National Criminal Justice Training Center

The National Criminal Justice Training Center (NCJTC) is a component of Fox Valley Technical College (FVTC) in Appleton, Wisconsin. NCJTC is one of the leading criminal justice training and educational organizations in the United States, using the skills and abilities of more than 300 experienced criminal justice professionals to provide training and technical assistance. Since 1968, hundreds of thousands of professionals from federal, state, tribal, and local law enforcement; criminal justice; and service provider agencies in the United States have benefited from NCJTC's assistance.

To meet the unique training and technical assistance needs of law enforcement and criminal justice practitioners, NCTC designs, develops, and conducts training throughout United States and internationally. The center has coordinated some of the nation's largest training events, including the 2010 Project Safe Childhood National Conference, the 2012 Office for Victims of Crime (OVC) Mass Casualty Conference, and the Internet Crimes Against Children (ICAC) National Training Conferences.

Since 2002, NCJTC provided training and technical assistance for tribal communities located throughout the country, including Alaska. NCJTC works with staff, subject matter experts, and partners to support the unique and diverse needs of American Indian and Alaska Native tribes. This includes training on community policing, community safety, alcohol and substance abuse, Native gangs, tribal probation, defensive tactics, courthouse security, community capacity building, strategic planning, sex offender management, and child protection in Indian Country training. In addition, NCJTC coordinates national conferences for tribal service providers, including the American Indian Justice Conference, the National Training Conference for Criminal Justice and Community Leaders, and the Crimes Against Children in Indian Country Conference.

In 2008, the COPS Office selected NCJTC to serve as the training and technical assistance provider for the office's FY2008 Tribal Resources Grant Program (TRGP) recipients to help grantees identify and address community safety concerns through community oriented policing practices.

Additional information regarding NCJTC can be found at www.NCJTC.org.